FIERCE
ATTACHMENTS

A MEMOIR

VIVIAN GORNICK

A TOUCHSTONE BOOK
Published by Simon & Schuster Inc.
NEW YORK • LONDON • TORONTO • SYDNEY • TOKYO

Copyright © 1987 by Vivian Gornick

First Touchstone Edition, 1988

Published by Simon & Schuster Inc.
Simon & Schuster Building
Rockefeller Center
1230 Avenue of the Americas
New York, New York 10020

Published by arrangement with Farrar, Straus & Giroux

TOUCHSTONE and colophon are registered trademarks
of Simon & Schuster Inc.

Manufactured in the United States of America

10 9 8 7 6 5 4 3 2   Pbk.

Library of Congress Cataloging in Publication Data

Gornick, Vivian.
    Fierce attachments: a memoir / Vivian Gornick.
        p. cm.— (A Touchstone Book)
    Reprint. Originally published: New York: Farrar Straus Giroux,
© 1987.
    ISBN 0-671-65757-7 Pbk.
    1. Gornick, Vivian. 2. Daughters—New York (N.Y.)—Biography.
3. Jews—New York (N.Y.)—Biography. 4. Mothers and daughters—
New York (N.Y.)—Case studies. I. Title.
HQ755.85.G67 1988   974.7'104'0924—dc19 [B]   87-37637

FIERCE ATTACHMENTS

February, 1989

To Betsy,
    I love your
courage, your dedication
and your love for your
mother.

            Always,

                Catriona

I'm eight years old. My mother and I come out of our apartment onto the second-floor landing. Mrs. Drucker is standing in the open doorway of the apartment next door, smoking a cigarette. My mother locks the door and says to her, "What are you doing here?" Mrs. Drucker jerks her head backward toward her own apartment. "He wants to lay me. I told him he's gotta take a shower before he can touch me." I know that "he" is her husband. "He" is always the husband. "Why? He's so dirty?" my mother says. "He feels dirty to *me*," Mrs. Drucker says. "Drucker, you're a whore," my mother says. Mrs. Drucker shrugs her shoulder. "I can't ride the subway," she says. In the Bronx "ride the subway" was a euphemism for going to work.

I lived in that tenement between the ages of six and twenty-one. There were twenty apartments, four to a floor, and all I remember is a building full of women. I hardly remember the men at all. They were everywhere, of course—husbands, fathers, brothers—but I remember only the women. And I remember them all crude like Mrs. Drucker or fierce like my mother. They never spoke as though they knew who they were, understood the bargain they had struck

3

with life, but they often acted as though they knew. Shrewd, volatile, unlettered, they performed on a Dreiserian scale. There would be years of apparent calm, then suddenly an outbreak of panic and wildness: two or three lives scarred (perhaps ruined), and the turmoil would subside. Once again: sullen quiet, erotic torpor, the ordinariness of daily denial. And I—the girl growing in their midst, being made in their image—I absorbed them as I would chloroform on a cloth laid against my face. It has taken me thirty years to understand how much of them I understood.

My mother and I are out walking. I ask if she remembers the women in that building in the Bronx. "Of course," she replies. I tell her I've always thought sexual rage was what made them so crazy. "Absolutely," she says without breaking her stride. "Remember Drucker? She used to say if she didn't smoke a cigarette while she was having intercourse with her husband she'd throw herself out the window. And Zimmerman, on the other side of us? They married her off to him when she was sixteen, she hated his guts, she used to say if he'd get killed on the job (he was a construction worker) it would be a *mitzvah*." My mother stops walking. Her voice drops in awe of her own memory. "He actually used to take her by physical force," she says. "Would pick her up in the middle of the living-room floor and carry her off to the bed." She stares into the middle distance for a moment. Then she says to me,

4

"The European men. They were animals. Just plain animals." She starts walking again. "Once, Zimmerman locked him out of the house. He rang our bell. He could hardly look at me. He asked if he could use our fire-escape window. I didn't speak one word to him. He walked through the house and climbed out the window." My mother laughs. "That fire-escape window, it did some business! Remember Cessa upstairs? Oh no, you couldn't remember her, she only lived there one year after we moved into the house, then the Russians were in that apartment. Cessa and I were very friendly. It's so strange, when I come to think of it. We hardly knew each other, any of us, sometimes we didn't talk to each other at all. But we lived on top of one another, we were in and out of each other's house. Everybody knew everything in no time at all. A few months in the building and the women were, well, *intimate.*

"This Cessa. She was a beautiful young woman, married only a few years. She didn't love her husband. She didn't hate him, either. He was a nice man, actually. What can I tell you, she didn't love him, she used to go out every day, I think she had a lover somewhere. Anyway, she had long black hair down to her ass. One day she cut it off. She wanted to be modern. Her husband didn't say anything to her, but her father came into the house, took one look at her cut hair, and gave her a slap across the face she saw her grandmother from the next world. Then he instructed her husband to lock her in the house for a month. She used to come down the fire escape into my window and out my door. Every afternoon for a month. One day she comes back and we're having coffee in the kitchen. I say to her, 'Cessa, tell your father this is America, Cessa, America. You're a free woman.' She looks at me and she says to me, 'What do you mean, tell my father this is America? He was born in Brooklyn.' "

My relationship with my mother is not good, and as our lives accumulate it often seems to worsen. We are locked into a narrow channel of acquaintance, intense and binding. For years at a time there is an exhaustion, a kind of softening, between us. Then the rage comes up again, hot and clear, erotic in its power to compel attention. These days it is bad between us. My mother's way of "dealing" with the bad times is to accuse me loudly and publicly of the truth. Whenever she sees me she says, "You hate me. I know you hate me." I'll be visiting her and she'll say to anyone who happens to be in the room—a neighbor, a friend, my brother, one of my nieces—"She hates me. What she has against me I don't know, but she hates me." She is equally capable of stopping a stranger on the street when we're out walking and saying, "This is my daughter. She hates me." Then she'll turn to me and plead, "What did I do to you, you should hate me so?" I never answer. I know she's burning and I'm glad to let her burn. Why not? I'm burning, too.

But we walk the streets of New York together endlessly. We both live in lower Manhattan now, our apartments a mile apart, and we visit best by walking. My mother is an urban peasant and I am my mother's daughter. The city is our natural element. We each have daily adventures with bus drivers, bag ladies, ticket takers, and street crazies. Walking brings out the best in us. I am forty-five now and my mother is seventy-seven. Her body is strong and healthy. She traverses the island easily with me. We don't love each other on these walks, often we are raging at each other, but we walk anyway.

Our best times together are when we speak of the past. I'll say to her, "Ma, remember Mrs. Kornfeld? Tell me that story again," and she'll delight in telling me the story again. (It is only the present she hates; as soon as the present becomes the past, she immediately begins loving it.) Each time she tells the story it is both the same and different because each time I'm older, and it occurs to me to ask a question I didn't ask the last time around.

The first time my mother told me that her uncle Sol had tried to sleep with her I was twenty-two and I listened silently: rapt and terrified. The background I knew by heart. She was the youngest of eighteen children, eight of whom survived into adult life. (Imagine. My grandmother was pregnant for twenty years.) When the family came to New York from Russia, Sol, my grandmother's youngest brother and the same age as her own oldest child (her mother had *also* been pregnant for twenty years), came along with them. My mother's two oldest brothers had preceded the family by some years, had gone to work in the rag trade, and had rented a cold-water flat on the Lower East Side for all eleven of them: bathroom in the hall, coal stove in the kitchen, a train of dark cubbyhole inner rooms. My mother, then a ten-year-old child, slept on two chairs in the kitchen, because my grandmother took in a boarder.

7

Sol had been drafted into the army during the First World War and sent to Europe. When he returned to New York my mother was sixteen years old and the only child left at home. So here he comes, a glamorous stranger, the baby niece he left behind now womanly and dark-eyed, with glossy brown hair cut in a stylish bob and a transforming smile, all of which she pretends she doesn't know how to use (that was always my mother's style: outrageous coquettishness unhampered by the slightest degree of self-consciousness), and he begins sleeping in one of those cubbyholes two walls away from her, with the parents snoring loudly at the farthest end of the apartment.

"One night," my mother said, "I jumped up from sleep, I don't know why, and I see Sol is standing over me. I started to say, 'What is it?' I thought something was wrong with my parents, but then he looked so funny I thought maybe he was sleepwalking. He didn't say a word to me. He picked me up in his arms and he carried me to his bed. He laid us both down on the bed, and he held me in his arms, and he began to stroke my body. Then he lifted my nightgown and he began to stroke my thigh. Suddenly he pushed me away from him and said, 'Go back to your bed.' I got up and went back to my bed. He never spoke one word about what happened that night, and I didn't either."

The second time I heard the story I was thirty. She repeated it nearly word for word as we were walking up Lexington Avenue somewhere in the Sixties. When she came to the end I said to her, "And you didn't say anything to him, throughout the whole time?" She shook her head no. "How come, Ma?" I asked. Her eyes widened, her mouth ·

8

pursed. "I don't know," she puzzled. "I only know I was very scared." I looked at her, as she would say, *funny*. "Whatsamatter?" she said. "You don't like my answer?" "No," I protested, "it's not that. It just seems odd not to have uttered a sound, not to have indicated your fears at all."

The third time she told the story I was nearly forty. We were walking up Eighth Avenue, and as we neared Forty-second Street I said to her, "Ma, did it ever occur to you to ask yourself *why* you remained silent when Sol made his move?" She looked quickly at me. But this time she was wise to me. "What are you getting at?" she asked angrily. "Are you trying to say I *liked* it? Is that what you're getting at?" I laughed nervously, gleefully. "No, Ma, I'm not saying that. I'm just saying it's *odd* that you didn't make a sound." Again, she repeated that she had been very frightened. "Come off it," I said sharply. "You are disgusting!" she raged at me in the middle of the street. "My brilliant daughter. I should send you to college for another two degrees you're so brilliant. I *wanted* my uncle to rape me, is that it? A new thought!" We didn't speak for a month after that walk.

The Bronx was a patchwork of invaded ethnic territories: four or five square blocks dominated by Irish or Italians or Jews, but each section with its quota of Irish living in a Jewish block or Jews in an Italian block. Much has been made of this change rung on the New York neighborhood register, but those who grew up running the Irish or Italian gauntlet, or being frozen out by Jewish neighbors, are not nearly so marked by their extra portion of outsidedness as they are leveled by the shared street life. Our family had lived for a year in an Italian neighborhood. My brother and I had been the only Jewish children in the school, and we had indeed been miserable. That's all: miserable. When we moved back into a Jewish neighborhood, my brother was relieved at no longer having to worry that he'd be beaten up every afternoon by kids who called him the Jewish genius, but the outline and substance of his life were not fundamentally altered. The larger truth is that the "otherness" of the Italians or the Irish or the Jews among us lent spice and interest, a sense of definition, an exciting edge to things that was openly feared but secretly welcomed.

Our building was all Jewish except for one Irish family on the first floor, one Russian family on the third floor, and a Polish superintendent. The Russians were tall and silent: they came and went in the building in a manner that seemed mysterious. The Irish were all thin and blond: blue eyes, narrow lips, closed faces. They, too, were a shadowy presence among us. The super and his wife were also quiet. They never spoke first to anyone. That's the main thing, I guess, about being a few among the many: it silences you.

My mother might have been silenced, too, had she remained living among the Italians, might have snatched her children up in wordless anxiety when a neighbor befriended one of us, just as Mrs. Cassidy did whenever a

10

woman in our building smoothed the hair of one of the "Irish blondies." But my mother was not one among the many. Here, in this all-Jewish building, she was in her element, had enough room between the skin of social presence and the flesh of an unknowing center in which to move around, express herself freely, be warm and sarcastic, hysterical and generous, ironic and judgmental, and, occasionally, what she thought of as affectionate: that rough, bullying style she assumed when overcome with the tenderness she most feared.

My mother was distinguished in the building by her unaccented English and the certainty of her manner. Although our apartment door was always closed (a distinction was made between those educated enough to value the privacy of a closed door and those so peasant-like the door was always half open), the neighbors felt free to knock at any time: borrow small kitchen necessities, share a piece of building gossip, even ask my mother to act as arbiter in an occasional quarrel. Her manner at such times was that of a superior person embarrassed by the childlike behavior of her inferiors. "Oy, Zimmerman." She would smile patronizingly when Mrs. Zimmerman, beside herself over some slight, real or imagined, came to tell her of the perfidy of one or another of our neighbors. "Such foolishness." Or, "That's ridiculous," she would rap out sharply when a tale she considered base or ignorant was repeated to her. She seemed never to be troubled by the notion that there might be two sides to a story, or more than one interpretation of an event. She knew that, compared with the women around her, she was "developed"—a person of higher thought and feeling—so what was there to think about? "Developed" was one of her favorite words. If Mrs. Zimmerman spoke loudly in the hall on a Saturday morning, we, sitting in the kitchen just behind our apartment door, would stare at each other and, inevitably, my mother would shake her head and pronounce, "An undeveloped woman." If someone made a crack about the *schvartzes,* my mother would carefully explain to me that such sentiments were "undeveloped." If there was a dispute in the grocery store over price or weight, again I would hear the word "undeveloped." My father smiled at her when she said "undeveloped," whether out of indulgence or pride I never did know. My brother, on his guard from the age of ten, stared without expression. But I, I absorbed the feel of her words, soaked up every accompanying gesture and expression, every complicated bit of impulse and intent. Mama thinking everyone around was undeveloped, and most of what they said was ridiculous, became imprinted on me like dye on the most receptive of materials.

The apartment was a five-room flat, with all the rooms opening onto each other. It was a tenement flat not a railroad flat: not one window looked into an airshaft. The apartment door opened into a tiny foyer that gave directly onto the kitchen. To the right of the kitchen, in the foyer, stood the refrigerator, propped against a wall at right angles to the bathroom: a tiny rectangle with a painted wooden door whose upper half was frosted glass. Beyond the foyer stood two rooms of equal size separated by a pair of curtained glass doors. The second of these rooms faced the street and was flooded with afternoon sunlight. Off this front room, at either end, were two tiny bedrooms, one of which also faced the street, the other the back of the building.

Because the front room and one of the bedrooms faced the street, ours was considered a desirable apartment, an apartment "to the front." A few years ago a man who had also grown up on my block said to me, "I always thought you were richer than us because you lived to the front." Although living to the front usually did mean that the husbands made more money than did the husbands of those living *tief, teier in draird* (deeply, dearly in hell) to the back, we lived to the front because part of my mother's claim to a superior grasp of life's necessities rested on her insistence that, unless we stood nose to nose with welfare, an apartment to the back was not within the range of domestic consideration. Nevertheless, it was "to the back" that we—that is, she and I—actually lived.

The kitchen window faced the alley in the back of the building, as did the kitchen windows of the building next to ours, and those of two other buildings whose entrances were on the opposite side of the square block these apartment houses shared. There were no trees or bushes or grasses of any kind in the alley—only concrete, wire fencing, and wooden poles. Yet I remember the alley as a place of clear light and sweet air, suffused, somehow, with a perpetual smell of summery green.

The alley caught the morning sun (our kitchen was radiant before noon), and it was a shared ritual among the women that laundry was done early on a washboard in the sink and hung out to dry in the sun. Crisscrossing the alley, from first floor to fifth, were perhaps fifty

13

clotheslines strung out on tall wooden poles planted in the concrete ground. Each apartment had its own line stretching out among ten others on the pole. The wash from each line often interfered with the free flap of the wash on the line above or below, and the sight of a woman yanking hard at a clothesline, trying to shake her wash free from an indiscriminate tangle of sheets and trousers, was common. While she was pulling at the line she might also be calling "Berth-a-a. Berth-a-a. Ya home, Bertha?" Friends were scattered throughout the buildings on the alley, and called to one another all during the day to make various arrangements ("What time ya taking Harvey to the doctor?" Or, "Got sugar in the house? I'll send Marilyn over." Or, "Meetcha on the corner in ten minutes"). So much stir and animation! The clear air, the unshadowed light, the women calling to each other, the sounds of their voices mixed with the smell of clothes drying in the sun, all that texture and color swaying in open space. I leaned out the kitchen window with a sense of expectancy I can still taste in my mouth, and that taste is colored a tender and brilliant green.

For me, the excitement in the apartment was located in the kitchen and the life outside its window. It was a true excitement: it grew out of contradiction. Here in the kitchen I did my homework and kept my mother company, watched her prepare and execute her day. Here, also, I learned that she had the skill and vitality to do her work easily and well but that she disliked it, and set no store by it. She taught me nothing. I never learned how to cook, clean, or iron clothes. She herself was a boringly competent cook, a furiously fast housecleaner, a demonic washerwoman.

Still, she and I occupied the kitchen fully. Although my mother never seemed to be listening to what went on in the alley, she missed nothing. She heard every voice, every motion of the clothesline, every flap of the sheets, registered each call and communication. We laughed together over this one's broken English, that one's loudmouthed indiscretion, a screech here, a fabulous curse there. Her running commentary on the life outside the window was my first taste of the fruits of intelligence: she knew how to convert gossip into knowledge. She would hear a voice go up one octave and observe: "She had a fight with her husband this morning." Or it would go down an octave and, "Her kid's sick." Or she'd catch a fast exchange and diagnose a cooling friendship. This skill of hers warmed and excited me. Life seemed fuller, richer, more interesting when she was making sense of the human activity in the alley. I felt a live connection, then, between us and the world outside the window.

The kitchen, the window, the alley. It was the atmosphere in which she was rooted, the background against which she stood outlined. Here she was smart, funny, and energetic, could exercise authority and have impact. But she felt contempt for her environment. "Women, yech!" she'd say. "Clotheslines and gossip," she'd say. She knew there was another world—*the* world—and sometimes she thought she wanted that world. Bad. She'd stop dead in the middle of a task, staring for long minutes at a time at the sink, the floor, the stove. But where? how? what?

So this was her condition: here in the kitchen she knew who she was, here in the kitchen she was restless and bored,

15

here in the kitchen she functioned admirably, here in the kitchen she despised what she did. She would become angry over the "emptiness of a woman's life" as she called it, then laugh with a delight I can still hear when she analyzed some complicated bit of business going on in the alley. Passive in the morning, rebellious in the afternoon, she was made and unmade daily. She fastened hungrily on the only substance available to her, became affectionate toward her own animation, then felt like a collaborator. How could she not be devoted to a life of such intense division? And how could I not be devoted to her devotion?

"Do you remember the Rosemans?" my mother asks as we are walking up Sixth Avenue in the Forties. They were the family who lived in the Zimmerman apartment our first two years in the building.

"Of course," I say. "Now *they* were an interesting couple."

Mrs. Roseman was a Jewish Colette: fat and swarthy, with long dark eyes in a beautiful fox face and an aureole of gray-black kinky hair. She played cards obsessively, chain-smoked, and was openly uninterested in her family. There was always a card game going in her house and, as my mother said, "a pot of some kind of shit cooking on the stove all day long, by the time her husband came home from work it tasted like my grandmother's old shoes." But my mother's voice was affectionate not indicting. She was

16

attached to Mrs. Roseman because she, too, had been a member of Tenants' Council Number 29 ten years earlier in a building three neighborhoods away.

I had known since early childhood that my parents were fellow travelers of the Communist Party, and that of the two my mother had been the more politically active. By the time I was born she had stood on soapboxes in the Bronx pleading for economic and social justice. It was, in fact, part of her deprivation litany that if it hadn't been for the children she would have developed into a talented public speaker.

During the Depression the Communist Party sponsored and ran the Tenants' Councils, organizations formed to fight eviction for nonpayment of rent. My mother became the head of Tenants' Council Number 29 in the Bronx ("I was the only woman in the building who could speak English without an accent, so automatically I was voted head"), and continued to act as head until shortly after I was born, when my father made her "stop everything" to stay home with the baby. Until then, she said, she ran the council. Mama running the council was a childhood classic. "Every Saturday morning," she would tell me, the way other mothers told their children Mary had a little lamb, "I would go down to Communist Party headquarters in Union Square and receive my instructions for the week. Then we would organize, and carry on." How she loved saying, "Then we would organize, and carry on." There was more uncomplicated pleasure in her voice when she repeated those words than in any others I ever heard her speak.

Tenants' Council Number 29 was made up of most of the women in the building my parents were then living in:

17

immigrant Jews, coarse and energetic. Tenement intimacy among them was compounded by political comradeship. When we had moved into this, our final building in the Bronx, and my mother found Mrs. Roseman living next door, it was as though she had unexpectedly come across not an old friend but a member of a family in whose presence she had once been surprised by complicated stirrings of her own mind and spirit. She and Mrs. Roseman each appreciated the other's ability to understand political activity that had tapped a reservoir of strong feeling.

One particular memory of their time together in the council, remarkably unpolitical by their own lights, held them both, and they reminisced often about this incident, always with much head shaking and in an atmosphere of shared wonderment. In the middle of the Depression the women of the council rented rooms one summer, for themselves and their families, in a bungalow colony in the Catskill Mountains. Most of the families had taken two rooms in the main building (one for the husband and wife, one for the children), although some could manage only one. The women shared the kitchen, the men came up on weekends.

They were fifteen women, and as my mother said, there in that kitchen she got to know them better than in the two or three years they'd been working together in the Bronx. There was Pessy, she said, "so stupid, put shit on the table she'd call it honey, but a good comrade, no matter what I told her to do she did it without hesitation or complaint." There was Singer, "the delicate type," she hated the vulgarity of the others. There was Kornfeld, "a dark and passionate-looking woman, never offered an opinion, al-

18

ways waited until everyone else spoke, then had to be asked what she thought, but always had something intelligent to say." And, of course, there was Roseman, shrewd, easy-going Roseman, who never missed a trick. Her eyes were everywhere at once, all the while she was dealing cards.

That summer my mother discovered that Pessy had "a real appetite, you know what I mean?" And Singer turned out to be a pain in the ass. "She was always fainting. No matter what happened, Singer's eyes would start rolling, and she was going under." And Kornfeld, well, Kornfeld was another story.

On Saturday, late in the morning, Pessy would come down in her nightgown, yawning and rubbing herself. The others would start laughing. "Well, Pessy," someone would say, "tell us what you did last night. You did something good?" Pessy would snort, "What's to tell? You do what you have to do, then you turn yourselves ass to ass, and you go to sleep. What do you want me to tell you?" But she'd be red-faced and smiling like she had a secret. Singer would turn her face away. And Kornfeld, she'd be sitting in a corner of the kitchen (she was one of those too poor for two rooms, they slept in one room with the three children), she would get more quiet than usual.

One Sunday night, after the men had gone back to the city and the women were all sitting on the porch, some-body suddenly said, "Where's Kornfeld?" They looked around, sure enough, no Kornfeld. They started calling, "Kornfeld, Kornfeld." No answer. They went into her room, the children were sound asleep, but no Kornfeld. They got frightened and began to search for her. They fanned out, two by two ("My luck," my mother said, "I got Singer"),

19

each with a flashlight ("You know how dark the country-side was in those years?"), and started yelling into the world, "Kornfeld, Kornfeld."

"An hour we must have been running around," my mother said, "like crazy people. Then I take a look and there, we're maybe half a mile from the farm, lying across the middle of the road, a black shape, not moving, you couldn't tell what it was. Right away, Singer starts fainting. I look from the road to Singer, from Singer to the road. 'Shut up, Singer,' I said. Then I turned to the thing in the road and I said, 'Get up, Kornfeld.' Singer's mouth opened and shut, but she didn't make a sound. The thing in the road didn't move. Again I said, 'Kornfeld, get up.' And then she got up. I turned Singer around and walked her back to the farm."

"How did you know it was Mrs. Kornfeld?" I asked the first time I heard the story. "I don't know," my mother said, "I just knew. I knew *immediately*." Another time I asked, "Why do you think she did it?" My mother shrugged. "She was a passionate woman. You know, Jews weren't so bold forty years ago, like some people I could name, they didn't have sex with the children in the room . . . Maybe she wanted to punish us." Another year my mother startled me by saying, "That Kornfeld. She hated herself. That's why she did it." I asked her to explain what she meant by "hated herself." She couldn't.

But what I have always remembered most about the Kornfeld story was that Mrs. Roseman, who gave off more sexual shrewdness than all the women in the building put together, and considered my mother a working-class romantic, had respected her because she'd known the thing in the road was Kornfeld.

"Do you remember the girls?" my mother asks now, as we are approaching the Time-Life Building. "The two daughters she had by Roseman?" Mrs. Roseman had had a lover when she was young, an Italian Communist who had died and left her pregnant. Mr. Roseman had adored her, married her, raised the child (a boy) as though he were his own, and had then fathered two children himself.

"Yes," I say. "I remember the girls."

"Do you remember that during the war the younger one, she must have been seventeen then, got pneumonia? They thought she was dying, in those years people died of pneumonia, and I bought her. After that she always called me Mama."

"You did *what?*" I stop walking.

"I bought her, I bought her. You know, Jews believed that if someone you loved was in danger you sold them and that warded off the evil eye." She laughs. "If they weren't yours what could happen to them?"

I stare hard at her. She ignores my stare.

"Roseman came to the door and she said to me, 'The girl is dying. Will you buy her?' So I bought her. I think I gave Roseman ten dollars."

"Ma," I say, "you knew this was a peasant superstition, an old wives' tale, and still you took part in it? You agreed to buy her?"

"Of course I did."

"But, Ma! You were both *communists.*"

"Well, listen," she says. "We had to save her life."

21

My parents slept, alternately, in either of the two middle rooms, some years in the back, some years in the front, whereupon the unused other room became the living room. For years they dragged a huge Philco radio and three monstrous pieces of furniture (an overstuffed couch and two chairs covered in maroon cloth threaded with gold) back and forth between the front room and the back room.

When I grew up I puzzled over why my parents had never taken one of the little rooms for themselves, why they slept in open territory, so to speak, and when I was in my twenties I asked my mother why. She looked at me just about thirty seconds too long. Then she said, "We knew that the children each needed a room for themselves." I gave her back the same thirty seconds. She had made such an intolerable romance of her marriage, had impaled us all on the cross of my father's early death, and here she was telling me that the privacy needed for sexual joy was given up for the good of the children?

My mother had been distinguished in the building not only by her unaccented English and the certainty of her manner, but also by her status as a happily married woman. No, I haven't said that right. Not just happily married. Magically married. Definitively married.

My parents were, I think, happy together, their behavior with one another civilized and affectionate—but an ideal of marital happiness suffused the atmosphere my mother and I shared that made simple reality a circumstance not worthy of respect, definitely not what it was all about. What it was all about was Mama's worshipful attitude toward the goodness of her married life, accompanied by a sniffing dismissal of all marriages that did not closely resemble hers, and the single-mindedness of her instruction to me in hundreds of ways, over thousands of days, that love was the most important thing in a woman's life.

Papa's love did indeed have wondrous properties: it not only compensated for her boredom and anxiety, it was the cause of her boredom and anxiety. Countless sentences having to do with all in her life she found less than satisfactory began: "Believe me, if I didn't love your father," or, "Believe me, if it wasn't for Papa's love." She would speak openly of how she had hated to give up working when she got married (she'd been a bookkeeper in a Lower East Side bakery), how good it was to have your own money in your pocket, not receive an allowance like a child, how stupid her life was now, and how she'd love to go back to work. Believe her. If it wasn't for Papa's love.

Everything from work in the kitchen to sex in the bedroom was transformed by Papa's love, and I think I knew early that sex did have to be transformed. She did not hate sex, but she did seem to put up with it. She never said physical love was unimportant or distasteful to a woman, but sentences like "Your father was a very passionate man. Your father was always ready. Your father could use ten women a night" left me feeling: To take your clothes off and lie down with a man you had to really really love him—otherwise the whole enterprise backfired. I remember at sixteen, my virginity under siege for the first time, waking each day to the interminable battle being waged in my head and my body, and imploring my mother silently: But, Ma, how do I know if I really really love him? All I know is, I'm in heat and he's pushing me, he's pushing me. In the hallway, on park benches, every night in the kitchen while you're tossing around on the other side of a wall eight feet away, safely behind the lines, I'm out here in the trenches . . . But there was no help forthcoming.

Love in my mother's lexicon wasn't love, it was *love*. Feeling of a high order, a spiritual nature, a moral cast. Above all, feeling that was unmistakable when present and equally unmistakable when absent. "A woman *knows* if she loves a man," my mother would say. "If she doesn't know she doesn't love him." These words were delivered as though from Sinai. Interpretation of the variety of human behaviors said to derive from love was not necessary in our house. If my mother could not identify in another woman responses to a husband or a lover that duplicated her own, it wasn't love. And love, she said, was everything. A woman's life was determined by love. All evidence to the contrary—and such evidence was abundant indeed—was consistently discounted and ignored, blotted out of her discourse, refused admission by her intellect. Once, in my presence (I must have been ten), a friend told her she was dead wrong, that her notions of love were absurd and that she was a slave to her idea of marriage. When I asked my mother what her friend meant she replied, "An undeveloped woman. She doesn't know life."

Every neighborhood had a village idiot or a holy fool; we had three. There was Tom, the sixty-year-old delivery boy who worked for the butcher. He'd carry a package of meat on the run, stop suddenly, throw the package down on the sidewalk, shake his finger at it, and announce: "I'm not going to carry you anymore, you lousy thing you!" There was Lilly, a mongoloid child of forty who wandered about in little-girl dresses, a pink satin bow in her greasy hair, crossing on the red light, cars screeching to a halt all around her. And there was Mrs. Kerner, a tiny, birdlike woman who ran around with her hair wrapped in a cleaning rag, her gestures wild, her manner crazily abrupt. She would stop people she didn't know in the grocery store or the butcher shop or at the druggist's, bring her hands together in a pair of loose fists in front of her face and, her brown eyes shining madly, say, "Oy, I was reading just today a bee-yoo-tee-ful story from Russian literature! A story of the heart to make the most miserable of souls cry out against the injustice of this life!" Then she would forget why she was in the store, turn and fly out the door.

Mrs. Kerner was Marilyn Kerner's mother. Marilyn was my best friend. The Kerners lived one floor below us, in the apartment next door, and were as different, my mother thought, from our family as it was possible to be. The difference eluded me. The Kerners were simply the family downstairs, and I thought: Well, that's how they do it in *their* house.

Marilyn was an only child. The Kerners had a three-room apartment. Marilyn and her mother slept on twin mahogany bedsteads in the bedroom; her father slept on a cot beside the couch in the living room. Mr. Kerner, like my father, worked in the garment district. He was a handsome, silent man with thick gray hair and cold blue eyes, who lived in my imagination as a perpetual source of fear and anxiety. His wife and daughter welcomed his departure and dreaded his arrival. His presence not only put an immediate stop to afternoon good times in the Kerner apartment, it was perceived as threatening. When Mrs. Kerner went stiff and alert at five-thirty, put her forefinger up in the air, and said, "Quiet! He's coming!" it was as though Bluebeard were about to walk through the door.

I preferred spending the afternoon in the Kerner apartment to spending it anywhere else. It was like having no parent in the house. Mrs. Kerner might be masquerading as an adult out on the street, but Marilyn and I knew better. With Mrs. Kerner it was so obvious that authority was an acquired position I began to suspect that perhaps more than one mother was assuming it, not earning it. Mrs. Kerner was enchanting and irritating: more interesting to be with than any regular mother, and more oddly instructive. My mother's presence was powerful, but Mrs. Kerner's was touching. Her distress was so open, so palpable, I would feel a finger pressing on my heart as she laid herself open to the ridicule and dismissal of a pair of street-smart twelve-year-olds.

She was a terrible housekeeper who never stopped keeping house. At all times she had a rag tied around her head, a feather duster in her hand, and an expression of confusion in her eyes. She would wander around the house, aimlessly flicking the duster here and there. Or she'd drag out an iron monster of a vacuum cleaner, start it up with a terrific whining noise that made you think a plane was about to land in the living room, push it across the threadbare carpet a few times, lose interest, and leave the vacuum cleaner standing where she turned it off, sometimes for two or three days.

She baked also: the most godawful stuff, a kind of breadcake loaf, always the same unyielding mass of half-raw dough. She'd break off a piece, lift it dramatically to her nose, inhale deeply, declare it ambrosia, and feed it to me or Marilyn. "Tasty, isn't it?" she'd say, beaming, and I'd nod, chewing as fast as I could to get it down (that took a good three, four minutes), knowing it would weigh on my chest for the rest of the day. But I wanted to get it down. I knew Mrs. Kerner would be more confused than usual if I didn't (what was she doing wrong now?), and I think I felt protective toward her from our earliest time together.

She never finished vacuuming because halfway through a push across the rug she would stop, jerk about (sometimes forgetting to turn off the machine), rush into the bedroom or the kitchen, where Marilyn and I were reading or drawing, and, with her hands on her face and her eyes shining, exclaim, "Oy, girls! Only this afternoon I was reading a story in the paper. A woman—poor, good, beautiful—was rushing across the street, her last penny in her hand to buy milk for a sick child she left upstairs, only a minute she left it, just to buy milk, a car comes rushing around the corner, hits her, knocks her down, crushes and destroys her. A *gevalt!* People come running. Blood everywhere! The world is drenched in her blood. They take her away. And guess what? You'll never believe this. It is impossible that the human mind should have imagined what actually happened. Are you ready? An hour later they find her hand in the gutter. Still clutching the penny."

Marilyn, if she was drawing, would forget to put down her charcoal stick. I, if I was reading, would remain sitting with a page between my fingers. Irritated at first by her appearance in the doorway, we invariably found ourselves drawn in by her urgent, lilting voice. My heart would beat faster as she spoke, my attention press itself against the unexpectedness of her details. Mrs. Kerner was a spellbinder. Hers was the power of the born storyteller—that is, the one for whom every scrap of experience is only waiting to be given shape and meaning through the miracle of narrative speech.

It wasn't a philosophic need to make sense of it all that drove Mrs. Kerner to storytelling. It was, rather, that she treasured feeling, and for her the arts—music, painting, literature—were a conduit for pure emotion. She told stories because she pined to live in a world of beauty among cultured people who had feeling. And feeling, girls, was everything. A person's life was made rich or poor, worth a ransom or something to throw away in the gutter, if it was enhanced by or stripped of feeling.

Mrs. Kerner would generally deliver this impassioned speech about art, life, and feeling after she had told us a story. Sometimes she would then push up her sleeves and run to the piano, which had been bought for forty dollars over Mr. Kerner's protest so that Marilyn who hated it, never touched it, would be able to bring into the house, right into the house, Chopin, Rachmaninoff, Mozart. The piano stood unused in the foyer except for the two or three times a week Mrs. Kerner rushed at it, wiped the bench with her skirt, sat down with the exaggerated motions of an artist at the piano, raised her arms high in the air, and brought her fingers down hard into the opening bars of "The Volga Boatmen." That was it. That was all she could play. The opening bars of "The Volga Boatmen." These she repeated ten or twenty times with no diminution of interest on either her part or ours.

The piano urge frequently overtook her during the last moments of the afternoon when, feverish with our shared storytelling rapture, she would lose track of the time. As she was crashing about on the piano keys the door would open and we would all freeze. Mr. Kerner would look silently at us. Then he would walk past us into the apartment, take a turn around the living room, come back into the foyer, hang his coat up carefully in the hall closet (he was the most fastidious man I ever knew), say, "The house is a pigpen. What have you been doing all day?" walk back into the living room, sit down in the one upholstered chair, and begin reading the paper. We would all scatter immediately: Mrs. Kerner to the kitchen, Marilyn to the bedroom, I out the door.

One Saturday morning Marilyn and I were on our way to Tremont Avenue, the major shopping street in our neighborhood. Just out the front door, Marilyn remembered that she had forgotten her wallet. We ran back upstairs, rushed into the Kerner apartment, and pushed into

29

the bedroom, Marilyn first me right behind her. She stopped abruptly on the threshold and I rammed into her. With my hands on her back I looked past her shoulder into the room. Mr. and Mrs. Kerner were in one of the mahogany bedsteads, he on top of her, both of them covered with a blanket, only their naked upper bodies visible. His face was buried, hers thrown back, her eyes closed, her mouth twisted in a silent moan. Her hands pressed strongly into his back, his mouth sucked at her neck. The convulsion was violent and, I knew instantly, mutual. A rush of heat and fear went through my body from my throat to my groin. It was that mutuality.

So there were the Kerners, riddled with hate, secretly locked together in sexual spasm, and there were my parents, loving each other, while their bed rode chastely about in open space. Downstairs the house was a shambles, the husband exiled to the living room, the wife a half-mad dreamer; upstairs all was barracks-clean, the husband at the fixed center, the wife impassioned and opinionated. These differences refused to imprint on me. They felt neither striking nor crucial. What did register was that both Mrs. Kerner and my mother adored romantic emotion, and both were married women.

We're walking up Fifth Avenue. It's a bad day for me. I'm feeling fat and lonely, trapped in my lousy life. I know I should be home working, and that I'm here playing the dutiful daughter only to avoid the desk. The anxiety is so great I'm walking with a stomachache. My mother, as always, knows she can do nothing for me, but my unhappiness makes her nervous. She is talking, talking at tedious, obfuscating length, about a cousin of mine who is considering divorce.

As we near the library an Eastern religionist (shaved head, translucent skin, a bag of bones wrapped in faded pink gauze) darts at us, a copy of his leader's writings extended in his hand. My mother keeps talking while the creature in gauze flaps around us, his spiel a steady buzz in the air, competing for my attention. At last, she feels interrupted. She turns to him. "What *is* it?" she says. "What do you want from me? Tell me." He tells her. She hears him out. Then she straightens her shoulders, draws herself up to her full five feet two inches, and announces: "Young man, I am a Jew and a socialist. I think that's more than enough for one lifetime, don't you?" The pink-gowned boy-man is charmed, and for a moment bemused. "My parents are Jews," he confides, "but they certainly aren't socialists." My mother stares at him, shakes her head, grasps my arm firmly in her fingers, and marches me off up the avenue.

"Can you believe this?" she says. "A nice Jewish boy

shaves his head and babbles in the street. A world full of crazies. Divorce everywhere, and if not divorce, *this*. What a generation you all are!"

"Don't start, Ma," I say. "I don't want to hear that bullshit again."

"Bullshit here, bullshit there," she says, "it's still true. Whatever else we did, we didn't fall apart in the streets like you're all doing. We had order, quiet, dignity. Families stayed together, and people lived decent lives."

"That's a crock. They didn't lead decent lives, they lived hidden lives. You're not going to tell me people were happier then, are you?"

"No," she capitulates instantly. "I'm not saying that."

"Well, what are you saying?"

She frowns and stops talking. Searches around in her head to find out what she is saying. Ah, she's got it. Triumphant, accusing, she says, "The unhappiness is so *alive* today."

Her words startle and gratify me. I feel pleasure when she says a true or a clever thing. I come close to loving her. "That's the first step, Ma," I say softly. "The unhappiness has to be made alive before anything can happen."

She stops in front of the library. She doesn't want to hear what I'm saying, but she's excited by the exchange. Her faded brown eyes, dark and brilliant in my childhood, brighten as the meaning of her words and mine penetrates her thought. Her cheeks flush and her pudding-soft face hardens wonderfully with new definition. She looks beautiful to me. I know from experience she will remember this afternoon as a deeply pleasurable one. I also know she will not be able to tell anyone why it has been pleasurable.

She enjoys thinking, only she doesn't know it. She has never known it.

A year after my mother told Mrs. Drucker she was a whore the Druckers moved out of the building and Nettie Levine moved into their vacated apartment. I have no memory of the Druckers moving out or of Nettie moving in, no truck or moving van coming to take away or deposit the furniture, dishes, or clothes of the one or of the other. People and all their belongings seemed to evaporate out of an apartment, and others simply took their place. How early I absorbed the circumstantial nature of most attachments. After all, what difference did it really make if we called the next-door neighbor Roseman or Drucker or Zimmerman? It mattered only that there was a next-door neighbor. Nettie, however, would make a difference.

I was running down the stairs after school, rushing to get out on the street, when we collided in the darkened hallway. The brown paper bags in her arms went flying in all directions. We each said "Oh!" and stepped back, I against the staircase railing, she against the paint-blistered wall. I bent, blushing, to help her retrieve the bags scattered across the landing and saw that she had bright red hair piled high on her head in a pompadour and streaming down her back and over her shoulders. Her features were narrow and pointed (the eyes almond-shaped, the mouth and nose thin and sharp), and her shoulders were wide but she was slim. She reminded me of the pictures of Greta Garbo. My heart began to pound. I had never before seen a beautiful woman.

"Don't worry about the packages," she said to me. "Go out and play. The sun is shining. You mustn't waste it here in the dark. Go, go." Her English was accented, like the English of the other women in the building, but her voice was soft, almost musical, and her words took me by surprise. My mother had never urged me not to lose pleasure, even if it was only the pleasure of the sunny street. I ran down the staircase, excited. I knew she was the new neighbor. ("A *Ukrainishe* redhead married to a Jew," my mother had remarked dryly only two or three days before.)

Two evenings later, as we were finishing supper, the doorbell rang and I answered it. There she stood. "I . . . I . . ." She laughed, a broken, embarrassed laugh. "Your mother invited me." She looked different standing in the doorway, coarse and awkward, a peasant with a pretty face, not at all the gorgeous creature of the hallway. Immediately, I felt poised and generous. "Come in." I stepped courteously aside in the tiny foyer to let her pass into the kitchen.

"Sit down, sit down," my mother said in her rough-friendly voice, as distinguished from her rough I-really-mean-this voice. "Have a cup of coffee, a piece of pie." She pushed my brother. "Move over. Let Mrs. Levine sit down on the bench." A high-backed wooden bench ran the length of one side of the table; my brother and I each claimed a sprawling place on the bench as fast as we could.

"Perhaps you'd like a glass of schnapps?" My handsome,

gentle father smiled, proud that his wife was being so civil to a Gentile.

"Oh no," demurred Nettie, "it would make me dizzy. And please"—she turned ardently toward my mother—"call me Nettie, not Mrs. Levine."

My mother flushed, pleased and confused. As always, when uncertain she beat a quick retreat into insinuation. "I haven't seen Mr. Levine, have I," she said. In her own ears this was a neutral question, in anyone else's it was a flat statement bordering on accusation.

"No, you haven't." Nettie smiled. "He isn't here. Right now he's somewhere on the Pacific Ocean."

"*Oy vay,* he's in the army," my mother announced, the color beginning to leave her cheeks. It was the middle of the war. My brother was sixteen, my father in his late forties. My mother had been left in peace. Her guilt was extravagant.

"No," said Nettie, looking confused herself. "He's in the Merchant Marine." I don't think she fully understood the distinction. Certainly my mother didn't. She turned an inquiring face toward my father. He shrugged and looked blank.

"That's a seaman, Ma," my brother said quickly. "He works as a sailor, but he's not in the navy. He works on ships for private companies."

"But I thought Mr. Levine was Jewish," my mother protested innocently.

My brother's face brightened nearly to purple, but Nettie only smiled proudly. "He is," she said.

My mother dared not say what she wanted to say: Impossible! What Jew would work voluntarily on a ship?

35

Everything about Nettie proved to be impossible. She was a Gentile married to a Jew like no Jew we had ever known. Alone most of the time and apparently free to live wherever she chose, she had chosen to live among working-class Jews who offered her neither goods nor charity. A woman whose sexy good looks brought her darting glances of envy and curiosity, she seemed to value inordinately the life of every respectable dowd. She praised my mother lavishly for her housewifely skills—her ability to make small wages go far, always have the house smelling nice and the children content to be at home—as though these skills were a treasure, some precious dowry that had been denied her, and symbolized a life from which she had been shut out. My mother—secretly as amazed as everyone else by Nettie's allure—would look thoughtfully at her when she tried (often vaguely, incoherently) to speak of the differences between them, and would say to her, "But you're a wife now. You'll learn these things. It's nothing. There's nothing to learn." Nettie's face would then flush painfully, and she'd shake her head. My mother didn't understand, and she couldn't explain.

Rick Levine returned to New York two months after Nettie had moved into the building. She was wildly proud of her tall, dark, bearded seaman—showing him off in the street to the teenagers she had made friends with, dragging him in to meet us, making him go to the grocery store with her—and she became visibly transformed. A kind of illumination settled on her skin. Her green almond eyes were speckled with light. A new grace touched her movements: the way she walked, moved her hands, smoothed back her hair. There was suddenly about her an aristocracy

36

of physical being. Her beauty deepened. She was untouchable.

I saw the change in her, and was magnetized. I would wake up in the morning and wonder if I was going to run into her in the hall that day. If I didn't, I'd find an excuse to ring her bell. It wasn't that I wanted to see her with Rick: his was a sullen beauty, glum and lumpish, and there was nothing happening between them that interested me. It was *her* I wanted to see, only her. And I wanted to touch her. My hand was always threatening to shoot away from my body out toward her face, her arm, her side. I yearned toward her. She radiated a kind of promise I couldn't stay away from, I wanted . . . I wanted . . . I didn't know *what* I wanted.

But the elation was short-lived: hers and mine. One morning, a week after Rick's return, my mother ran into Nettie as they were both leaving the house. Nettie turned away from her.

"What's wrong?" my mother demanded. "Turn around. Let me see your face." Nettie turned toward her slowly. A tremendous blue-black splotch surrounded her half-closed right eye.

"Oh my God," my mother breathed reverently.

"He didn't mean it," Nettie pleaded. "It was a mistake. He wanted to go down to the bar to see his friends. I wouldn't let him go. It took a long time before he hit me."

After that she looked again as she had before he came home. Two weeks later Rick Levine was gone again, this time on a four-month cruise. He swore to his clinging wife that this would be his last trip. When he came home in April, he said, he would find a good job in the city and

37

they would at long last settle down. She believed that he meant it this time, and finally she let him pull her arms from around his neck. Six weeks after he had sailed she discovered she was pregnant. Late in the third month of his absence she received a telegram informing her that Rick had been shot to death during a quarrel in a bar in port somewhere on the Baltic Sea. His body was being shipped back to New York, and the insurance was in question.

Nettie became intertwined in the dailiness of our life so quickly it was hard later for me to remember what our days had been like before she lived next door. She'd slip in for coffee late in the morning, then again in the afternoon, and seemed to have supper with us three nights a week. Soon I felt free to walk into her house at any hour, and my brother was being consulted daily about the puzzling matter of Rick's insurance.

"It's a pity on her," my mother kept saying. "A widow. Pregnant, poor, abandoned."

Actually, her unexpected widowhood made Nettie safely pathetic and safely other. It was as though she had been trying, long before her husband died, to let my mother know that she was disenfranchised in a way Mama could never be, perched only temporarily on a landscape Mama was entrenched in, and when Rick obligingly got himself killed this deeper truth became apparent. My mother could now sustain Nettie's beauty without becoming unbalanced, and Nettie could help herself to Mama's respectability without being humbled. The compact was made

38

without a word between them. We got beautiful Nettie in the kitchen every day, and Nettie got my mother's protection in the building. When Mrs. Zimmerman rang our bell to inquire snidely after the *shiksa* my mother cut her off sharply, telling her she was busy and had no time to talk nonsense. After that no one in the building gossiped about Nettie in front of any of us.

My mother's loyalty once engaged was unswerving. Loyalty, however, did not prevent her from judging Nettie; it only made her voice her reservations in a manner rather more indirect than the one to which she was accustomed. She would sit in the kitchen with her sister, my aunt Sarah, who lived four blocks away, discussing the men who had begun to appear, one after another, at Nettie's door in the weeks following Rick's death. These men were his shipmates, particularly the ones who had been on board with him on this last voyage, coming to offer condolences to the widow of one of their own, and to talk over with her the matter of the seaman's life insurance, which evidently was being withheld from Nettie because of the way in which Rick had died. There was, my mother said archly, something *strange* about the way these men visited. Oh? My aunt raised an interested eyebrow. What exactly was strange? Well, my mother offered, some of them came only once, which was normal, but some of them came twice, three times, one day after another, and those who came two, three times had a look about them, she must surely be wrong about this, but they looked almost as though they thought they were getting away with something. And Nettie herself acted strangely with these men. Perhaps that was what was most troubling: the odd mannerisms Nettie seemed to adopt in the presence of the men. My mother and my aunt exchanged "glances."

"What do you mean?" I would ask loudly. "What's wrong with the way she acts? There's nothing wrong with the way she acts. Why are you talking like this?" They would become silent then, both of them, neither answering me nor talking again that day about Nettie, at least not while I was in the room.

One Saturday morning I walked into Nettie's house without knocking (her door was always closed but never locked). Her little kitchen table was propped against the wall beside the front door—her foyer was smaller than ours, you fell into the kitchen—and people seated at the table were quickly "caught" by anyone who entered without warning. That morning I saw a tall thin man with straw-colored hair sitting at the kitchen table. Opposite him sat Nettie, her head bent toward the cotton-print tablecloth I loved (we had shiny, boring oilcloth on our table). Her arm was stretched out, her hand lying quietly on the table. The man's hand, large and with great bony knuckles on it, covered hers. He was gazing at her bent head. I came flying through the door, a bundle of nine-year-old intrusive motion. She jumped in her seat, and her head came up swiftly. In her eyes was an expression I would see many times in the years ahead but was seeing that day for the first time, and although I had not the language to name it I had the sentience to feel jarred by it. She was calculating the impression this scene was making on me.

It's a cloudy afternoon in April, warm and gray, the air sweet with new spring. The kind of weather that induces nameless stirrings in unidentifiable parts. As it happens, it is also the anniversary of the Warsaw Ghetto uprising. My mother wants to attend the annual memorial meeting at Hunter College. She has asked me to come with her. I've refused, but I've agreed to walk her up Lexington Avenue to the school. Now, as we walk, she recounts an adventure she had yesterday on the street.

"I was standing on the avenue," she tells me, "waiting for the light to change, and a little girl, maybe seven years old, was standing next to me. All of a sudden, before the light changed, she stepped out into the street. I pulled her back onto the sidewalk and I said to her, 'Darling, never never cross on the red. Cross only on the green.' The kid looks at me with real pity in her face and she says, 'Lady, you've got it all upside down.'"

"That kid's not gonna make it to eight," I say.

"Just what I was thinking." My mother laughs.

We're on Lexington in the lower Forties. It's a Sunday. The street is deserted, its shops and restaurants closed, very few people out walking.

"I must have a cup of coffee," my mother announces.

My mother's wishes are simple but they are not negotiable. She experiences them as necessities. Right now she must have a cup of coffee. There will be no sidetracking

41

of this desire she calls a need until the cup of steaming liquid is in her hand being raised to her lips.

"Let's walk over to Third Avenue," I say. "There should be something open there." We cross the street and head east.

"I was talking to Bella this morning," my mother says on the other side of the avenue, shaking her head from side to side. "People are so cruel! I don't understand it. She has a son, a doctor, you should pardon me, he is so mean to her. I just don't understand. What would it hurt him, he'd invite his mother out for a Sunday to the country?"

"The country? I thought Bella's son works in Manhattan."

"He lives in Long Island."

"Is that the country?"

"It isn't West End Avenue!"

"Okay, okay, so what did he do now?"

"It isn't what he did now, it's what he does always. She was talking to her grandchild this morning and the kid told her they had a lot of people over yesterday afternoon, what a nice time they all had eating on the porch. You can imagine how Bella felt. She hasn't been invited there in months. Neither the son nor his wife have any feeling for her."

"Ma, how that son managed to survive having Bella for a mother, much less made it through medical school, is something for Ripley, and you know it."

"She's his mother."

"Oh, God."

"Don't 'oh, God' me. That's right. She's his mother. Plain and simple. She went without so that he could have."

"Have what? Her madness? Her anxiety?"

"Have life. Plain and simple. She gave him his life."

"That was all a long time ago, Ma. He can't remember that far back."

"It's uncivilized he shouldn't remember!"

"Be that as it may. It cannot make him want to ask her to sit down with his friends on a lovely Saturday afternoon in early spring."

"He should do it whether he wants to or not. Don't look at me like that. I know what I'm talking about."

We find a coffee shop on Third Avenue, an upwardly mobile greasy spoon, all plastic wood, vinyl leather, tin-plated chandeliers with candle-shaped bulbs burning in the pretentiously darkened afternoon.

"All right?" my mother says brightly to me.

If I said, "Ma, this place is awful," she'd say, "My fancy daughter. I was raised in a cold-water flat with the toilet in the hall but this isn't good enough for you. So okay, you pick the place," and we'd go trudging on up Third Avenue. But I nod yes, sit down with her in a booth by the window, and prepare to drink a cup of dreadful coffee while we go on with our weighty conversation about children and parents.

"Hot," my mother says to the heavy-lidded, black-haired waiter approaching our table very slowly. "I want my coffee hot."

He stares at her with so little expression on his face that each of us is sure he has not understood. Then he turns toward me, only his eyebrows inquiring. My mother puts her hand on his arm and cocking her head to one side smiles extravagantly at him. "Where are you from?" she asks.

"Ma," I say.

Holding the waiter fast between her fingers, she repeats, "Where?"

The waiter smiles. "Greek," he says to her. "I Greek."

"Greek," she says, as though assessing the value of the nationality he has offered her. "Good. I like Greeks. Remember. Hot. I want my coffee hot." He bursts out laughing. She's right. She knows what she's talking about. It's I who am confused in the world, not she.

Business over, she settles back into the argument. "It's no use. Say what you will, children don't love their parents as they did when I was young."

"Ma, do you really believe that?"

"I certainly do! My mother died in my sister's arms, with all her children around her. How will I die, will you please tell me? They probably won't find me for a week. Days pass. I don't hear from you. Your brother I see three times a year. The neighbors? Who? Who's there to check on me? Manhattan is not the Bronx, you know."

"Exactly. That's what this is all about. Manhattan is not the Bronx. Your mother didn't die in her daughter's arms because your sister loved her more than we love you. Your sister hated your mother, and you know it. She was there because it was her duty to be there, and because she lived around the corner all her married life. It had nothing to do with love. It wasn't a better life, it was an immigrant life, a working-class life, a life from another century."

44

"Call it what you want," she replies angrily, "it was a more human way to live."

We are silent. The waiter comes with the coffee. She has the cup in her hands before he has fully turned away. She sips, looks scornfully after his retreating back. "You think it's hot?" she says. "It's not hot."

"Call him back."

She pushes the air away with her hand. "Forget it. I'll drink it as it is, the devil won't take me." Clearly the conversation is depressing her.

"Well, all I can say is, if he wasn't her son Bella would never lay eyes on him again."

"That makes two of them, doesn't it? He certainly wouldn't lay eyes on her again if she wasn't his mother, would he?"

My mother gazes steadily at me across the table. "So what are you saying, my brilliant daughter?"

"I'm saying that nowadays love has to be earned. Even by mothers and sons."

Her mouth falls open and her eyes deepen with pity. What I have just said is so retarded she may not recover the power of speech. Then, shaking her head back and forth, she says, "I'll tell you like the kid told me, 'Lady, you've got the whole thing upside down.' "

At this moment the waiter passes by carrying a pot of steaming coffee. My mother's hand shoots out, nearly unbalancing him. "Is that hot?" she demands. "This wasn't hot." He shrugs, stops, pours coffee into her cup. She drinks greedily and nods grudgingly. "It's hot." Satisfaction at last.

"Let's go," she says, standing up, "it's getting late."

We retrace our steps and continue on up Lexington Avenue. The air is sweeter than before, warmer, fuller, with a hint of rain now at its bright gray edge. Delicious! A surge of expectation rises without warning in me but, as usual, does not get very far. Instead of coming up straight and clear it twists about, turns inward, and quickly stifles itself to death; a progress with which I am depressingly familiar. I glance sideways at my mother. I must be imagining this, but it seems to me her face reflects the same crazy journey of detoured emotion. There is color in her cheek, but her eye is startled and her mouth pulled downward. What, I wonder, does she see when she looks at me? The mood of the day begins to shift dangerously.

We're in the Fifties. Huge plate-glass windows filled with color and design line the avenue. What a relief it's Sunday, the stores are closed, no decisions to make. We share an appreciation of clothes, my mother and I, of looking nice in clothes, but we cannot bear to shop, either of us. We're always wearing the same few articles of clothing we have each picked hastily from the nearest rack. When we stand as we do now, before a store window, forced to realize there are women who dress with deliberation, we are aware of mutual disability, and we become what we often are: two women of remarkably similar inhibitions bonded together by virtue of having lived within each other's orbit nearly all their lives. In such moments the fact that we are mother and daughter strikes an alien note. I know it is precisely because we *are* mother and daughter that our responses are mirror images, yet the word filial does not seem appropriate. On the contrary, the idea of family, of our being family, of family *life* seems altogether puzzling: an uncertainty in her as well as in myself. We are so used to thinking of ourselves as a pair of women, ill-starred and incompetent (she widowed, me divorced), endlessly unable to get family life for themselves. Yet, as we stand before the store window, "family life" seems as much a piece of untested fantasy in her as it is in me. The clothes in the window make me feel we have both been confused the whole of our lives about who we are, and how to get there.

Suddenly, I am miserable. Acutely miserable. A surge of defeat passes through me. I feel desolated, without direction or focus, all my daily struggles small and disoriented. I become speechless. Not merely silent, but speechless. My mother sees that my spirits have plunged. She says nothing. We walk on, neither of us speaking.

We arrive at Sixty-ninth Street, turn the corner, and walk toward the entrance to the Hunter auditorium. The doors are open. Inside, two or three hundred Jews sit listening to the testimonials that commemorate their unspeakable history. These testimonials are the glue that binds. They remind and persuade. They heal and connect. Let people make sense of themselves. The speeches drone on. My mother and I stand there on the sidewalk, alone together, against the sound of culture-making that floats out to us. "We are a cursed people," the speaker announces. "Periodically we are destroyed, we struggle up again, we are reborn. That is our destiny."

The words act like adrenaline on my mother. Her cheeks begin to glow. Tears brighten her eyes. Her jawline grows firm. Her skin achieves muscle tone. "Come inside," she says softly to me, thinking to do me a good turn. "Come. You'll feel better."

I shake my head no. "Being Jewish can't help me anymore," I tell her.

She holds tightly to my arm. She neither confirms nor denies my words, only looks directly into my face. "Remember," she says. "You are my daughter. Strong. You must be strong."

"Oh Ma!" I cry, and my frightened greedy freedom-loving life wells up in me and spills down my soft-skinned face, the one she has given me.

Nettie gave birth on a miserably hot day in August after a fifty-hour labor that ripped her nearly in two. The baby was a twelve-pound boy. She named him Richard. From the moment my mother and I helped bring him back from the hospital, we began raising him alongside of and sometimes instead of Nettie herself. We gave him sustenance of various kinds, and from time to time we gave him his very life. He was a sickly infant, repeatedly developing an asthmatic croup that could be relieved only through the inhalation of steam heat. Invariably, it was my mother or my brother who sat under the improvised vaporizer (a towel-tent held over a pot of boiling water) with the gasping Richie, never Nettie who was rendered useless by all such crises. She would pace the floor and tear at her hair as soon as the baby began to wheeze.

Nettie, it quickly developed, had no gift for mothering. Many women have no gift for it. They mimic the recalled gestures and mannerisms of the women they've been trained to become and hope for the best. But Nettie had been trained to attract, not to domesticate, and was at a permanent loss. She could not master the art of mashed-up food, boiled diapers, baths in the kitchen sink. Her fingers remained clumsy, her movements inefficient, her mind unable to absorb the simplest scheme of organization. The kitchen stank of used diapers, the baby was wet and filthy, the sink crowded with unwashed pots coated in burnt milk. Nettie herself looked perpetually stunned. She was always turning around in the middle of the kitchen—legs bare, pompadour coming undone, brows drawn together in a frown, forefinger laid across her lips—trying to remember where she had mislaid some necessary thing or other . . . Now let me see, where *did* I put that baby?

Richie survived in a welter of muted confusion. I have this memory of him up in Nettie's right arm, his diaper full of shit, his face smeared with the remnants of the last two meals, his tiny fingers clutching a strand of red hair, holding on for dear life while she whirls about in silent alarm. Because she is silent it takes him awhile to become alarmed himself. There is in his face puzzled interest only slowly crumbling into panic.

Nettie's silence. That was another thing that separated her from the other women in the building. Among the others the first response to confusion or need was an explosion of high-decibel speech. Not so with Nettie. Her incapacity would have ingratiated her with the women, created a natural opening into their world—"Oh, teach me, tell me, is *that* how you do it, thank you, Mrs. Zimmerman-Roseman-Shapiro-Berger, you're so wise, I'm so ignorant, so glad to learn what you have to teach"—but she couldn't do it, didn't even know where to begin. She felt exposed before the women, remained silent, unconfiding, hiding her need from all of them. All except my mother.

My mother was Nettie's lifeline during that first year of Richie's life. It wasn't so much what Mama did for Nettie, although all the small bits of help (bringing home extra bread and milk, taking Richie for an hour, giving him a bath or a feed now and then) certainly eased Nettie's day. Mainly it was just that Mama was there to receive her anxiety. Periodically, Mama would wade into Nettie's kitchen and in two or three hours of concentrated labor make order and shining cleanliness. Then she'd turn to Nettie as though to say, "Now you're all set. Start your life." Nettie would beam at her, embrace and kiss her, and in three days the place would be exactly as it had been before. Nettie accepted my mother's labor not as a young woman might watching an older one in order to learn how to do it herself, but rather like a child being temporarily saved by a somewhat officious older sister. And indeed, Nettie sheltered with Richie as though they were both orphaned children: crooning at him, snuggling with him, hiding for days at a time with him under the bedclothes on the double bed that took up most of what was supposed to be the living room but wasn't.

Nettie's apartment was the smallest, darkest, most sparsely furnished in the building. The kitchen, which shared our view of the alley and our morning light, was the only pleasant room. Beyond it were two rooms of uneven size whose windows stared at a brick wall. One of these should have been the living room, the other the bedroom, but Nettie didn't know how to make a living room. The larger room held a double bed, a chest of drawers, a bit of shelving, and a rickety end table. The other room became a junk room, a large closet where the worst of her hopeless disorder could be pushed out of sight.

Yet to me the apartment, like Nettie herself, was touched with promise and allure. I didn't know the word beauty, would not have been able to say beauty was missing from our house; I only knew that small bits of visual pleasure transformed Nettie's tiny apartment, made me feel happy and expectant when I walked through her door. Motherhood had deranged her, upset her odd and lovely nesting habits, pitched her into chaos, but still: the bed was covered with a paisley spread of thin Ukrainian wool, a silver candelabrum stood on the rickety end table, an icon hung on the wall, the cardboard bridge table in the kitchen was hidden by a startling geometric-print cloth, and on the windowsill stood a large geranium plant always beautifully trimmed, its earth wet and black, its leaves deep green. On the darkest of days the brilliant red, black, and green of the plant was an excitement. It wasn't the objects themselves—we had a wonderful brass samovar in our living room I didn't notice until I was twenty-five—it was the way Nettie placed and arranged things, a gift she had for creating grace and beauty where there had been none before. And then of course there was the lace, everywhere Nettie's lace.

Nettie was a talented lacemaker. She had in fact been working in a lace factory when she met Rick Levine. She could make dresses and coats, cloths and spreads, but she never undertook such major enterprises. She only made doilies, pillow covers, antimacassars, small bits and pieces to brighten the tiny apartment. She never had a specific idea or a fixed design in mind when she sat down to make lace, she just worked at lace. She would sink into a chair at the kitchen table whenever Richie finally keeled over late in the afternoon or at night (he was never put to bed, he simply went unconscious), wind a length of the smooth, silky cotton thread around her wrist and forefinger, pick up the fine steel crochet hook, and begin. She worked to comfort herself, to entertain and mollify her ruffled spirits (there was no moment when Nettie wasn't recovering from motherhood). She did not take her talent seriously. If you watched her working you could see that it interested her— the designs seemed to emerge from her hook, they took her by surprise, she wanted to know how a piece of work would come out—but the interest was not sustained: one moment intent and concentrated, the next shrugged off, discarded, easily forgotten. Lacemaking was only a mildly valued companion, company when she was nervous or relaxed or hopeful or tense, winding up or winding down.

If I counted the hours I sat at the kitchen table while Nettie made lace, they would add up to a good two or three years. I was usually there in the late afternoon, and often in the evening after supper. She worked at the lace and I watched the movement of her hook, and we fell into a way of being together. She would fantasize out loud as she worked, and I would listen, actively, to her fantasizing.

"Wouldn't it be wonderful if . . ." was her ritual begin-

ning. From this sentence she would spin out a tale of rescue involving love or money as easily as she unwound the
silky thread from around her fingers. Like the plots of the
paperback romances she read (her lips moving as her eye
traveled slowly across the page), her fantasies were simple,
repetitious, and boring. The ones that turned on money
usually went: "Wouldn't it be wonderful if an old lady was
crossing the street and a truck nearly ran her down and I
saved her and she said, 'Oh my dear, how can I thank
you, here, take this,' and she gave me the necklace she
was wearing and I sold it for a thousand dollars." Or:
"Wouldn't it be wonderful if I was sitting on a bench in
the park and tucked between the slats was a brown paper
bag nobody would touch, it was so crumpled and dirty,
and I opened it and inside was a thousand dollars." (In the
late 1940s, in certain circles, a thousand was as good as a
million.)

The stories that turned on love were infinitely more ap-
pealing to her, and these she entered into with great clab-
oration: "Wouldn't it be wonderful if I'm coming off the
trolley car and I slip and sprain my ankle and they take
me to the hospital and the doctor who comes to help me
is tall and so handsome, and kind and gentle, and he looks
into my face and I look into his, and we can't tear our
eyes away from each other, it's as though we're glued together, we've been looking for each other all our lives and
now we're afraid to look away even for a minute, and he
says to me, 'I've been waiting such a long time for you,
will you marry me?' and I say, 'But you're a doctor, an
educated man, and I'm a poor woman, ignorant and un-

educated, I'll embarrass you,' and he says, 'I must have you, life is not worth living if I can't have you,' and that's it, we're together from then on."

Sometimes, after an hour or so of this, she would say to me, "Now you say what you'd like to have happen." And I would say, "Wouldn't it be wonderful if there was a flood or an epidemic or a revolution, and even though I'm this little kid they find me and they say to me, 'You speak so wonderfully you must lead the people out of this disaster.' " I never daydreamed about love or money, I always daydreamed I was making eloquent speeches that stirred ten thousand people to feel their lives, and to *act*.

Nettie would stare at me when I said what I would like to have happen. The sparkle in her eyes would flicker and her quick-moving fingers would drop into her lap. I think she was always hoping that *this* time it would be different, this time I'd come back with a story more like her own, one that made her feel good, not puzzled and awkward. But she must have known it was a long shot. Otherwise she would have asked me more often than she did to tell her what magic I longed for.

When I was fourteen years old, Nettie's lace figured strongly in a crucial development in my inner life. It was the year after my father's death, the year in which I began to sit on the fire escape late at night making up stories in my head. The atmosphere in our house had become morgue-like. My mother's grief was primitive and all-encompassing: it sucked the oxygen out of the air. A heavy drugged sensation filled my head and my body whenever I came back into the apartment. We, none of us—not my brother, not I, certainly not my mother—found comfort in one another. We were only exiled together, trapped in a common affliction. Loneliness of the spirit seized conscious hold of me for the first time, and I turned my face to the street, to the dreamy melancholy inner suggestiveness that had become the only relief from what I quickly perceived as a condition of loss, and of defeat.

I began sitting on the fire escape in the spring, and I sat there every night throughout that immeasurably long first summer, with my mother lying on the couch behind me moaning, crying, sometimes screaming late into the night, and my brother wandering aimlessly about, reading or pacing, the only conversation among us that of barely polite familiars: "Get me a glass of water," or, "Shut the window, there's a draft," or, "You going down? Bring back milk." I found I could make myself feel better simply by swinging my legs across the windowsill and turning my face fully outward, away from the room behind me.

The shabby tenement streets below our windows were transformed by darkness and silence. There was in the nighttime air a clarity, a softness and a fullness, indescribably sweet, that intensified the magical isolation I sought and that easily became a conduit for waking dreams. A hungry fantasizing went instantly to work as soon as I was seated with my back to the apartment, my eyes trained on the street. This fantasizing was only one step removed from Nettie's "Wouldn't it be wonderful," but it was an important step. Mine began "Just suppose," and was followed not by tales of immediate rescue but by imaginings of "large meaning." That is: things always ended badly but there was grandeur in the disaster. The point of my romances was precisely that life is tragic. To be "in tragedy" was to be saved from what I took to be the pedestrian pains of my own life. These seemed meaningless. To be saved from meaninglessness, I knew, was everything. Largeness of meaning was redemption. It was an adolescent writer's beginning: I had started to mythicize.

Late in the summer a woman I had never seen before appeared in the neighborhood, and began to walk up our block, late at night, across the street from the fire-escape window where I sat. I never saw her during the day, but she appeared promptly every night at eleven. She was thin and white-skinned. A mass of tangled black hair framed her face. Her shoulders were narrow and bony. She wore makeup and high heels. Her nylon stockings were loose and wrinkled around her ankles, and there was in her walk some muscular disconnect, as though she had been knocked apart like a puppet and put back together again badly. Sometimes she wore a thin shawl of tropical print. She was an altogether peculiar creature to have appeared on those streets, brimful as they were with working-class respectability, but I accepted her appearance as unthinkingly as I did the other human oddities on the block. Or at least I thought I did.

One night early in the fall as I was watching her walk jerkily up the block, I turned back into the living room where my brother was reading and my mother lying on the couch. I called my brother to the window and pointed to the woman in the street.

"Have you seen her?" I asked.

"Sure," he said.

56

"Who is she?"

"She's a prostitute."

"A what?"

"That's a person without a home," my mother said.

"Oh," I said.

In that moment I became aware that the woman on the street had moved me. I was stirred by her presence, her aspect. I felt her as a broken creature, broken and diseased, and I had begun to imagine myself healing her. This image now pushed through the scrim of half-conscious thought, and quickly developed itself. As I healed her she became changed, her shoulders widened, her skin cleared, her hair neatened; above all, her eyes became grave and purposeful. But still, the nights were growing colder and she shivered in her thin dress and torn shawl. I imagined myself draping her in some lovely material that was both warming and magically possessed of the power to increase the healing process. I couldn't see the material clearly for the longest time. Was it thin or thick, solid or print, light or dark? Then one night I looked closely at it and saw that it was lace. A series of flash images confused me. I saw Nettie's face cradled on a piece of her own lace. I saw myself and the prostitute and Nettie, all of us with our faces laid sadly against small pieces of lace. Not a mantle of lace for any one of us, only these bits and pieces, and all of us sorrowing against the bits and pieces.

We're walking west on Twenty-third Street. It's late in the day and hundreds of workers are streaming out of the Metropolitan Life Building. My mother, an expert walker in the city (not to mention seat-grabber on the subway), is elbowing her way free of the crowd, with me right behind her. She is making fair progress when a man places himself deliberately in her path. She moves to the left, he moves to the left. She moves to the right, he moves to the right. She stares into his chest and then quickly, like a frightened bird, up into his face: after all, this *is* New York. For a moment all systems of response shut down. She stops reacting. She is simply there. Then all at once she's in noisy operation again.

"Maddy!" she bursts out at the man. "Madison Shapiro. For God's sake!"

Now it's my turn to shut down. I know the name Maddy Shapiro very well, but I do not know the face in front of me. Ah, it hits me. It's not that I haven't seen Maddy Shapiro in more than twenty years, it's that Maddy Shapiro has had a nose job. I'm amazed that my mother spotted Maddy inside this newly arranged face of his.

The man standing in front of us is fifty years old. His tight curly hair is brown and gray, his eyes are cold blue, his figure beneath the well-cut business suit is thin and sexy, and he is made beautiful by the straight narrow line of a lovely nose: a nose not too long, not too short, just

58

right. In another life that nose was a painful Jewish droop, forever dragging everything in Maddy's sad young face down down down to the bottom of his soul. His mother, Mrs. Shapiro, who lived on the third floor of our building, was always running after him in the street with the glass of milk he wouldn't finish. The kids would scream, "Drink-your-milk-Maddy-drink-your-milk," and Maddy's nose would grow longer, and his mouth would pull downward into the sullen silence he adopted as a permanent means of survival.

When we were teenagers Maddy surprised us all one night at a neighborhood party with his extraordinary fox-trotting ("A regular Fred Astaire," my mother pronounced). Where had he learned to dance like that, we wondered. This was not the kind of dancing you learned from watching Astaire on Saturday afternoons in a darkened movie auditorium, or from moving about by yourself in front of the mirror. This dancing you got from *people*. But where? who? when? Did Maddy have a life somewhere *else*? The question was asked, but no one could wait for, much less pursue, an answer.

We hardly saw Maddy at all once he had begun high school, but one night when Marilyn Kerner and I were fooling around in my bedroom Maddy walked in and joined us. We began to play "What do you want your husband (or your wife, Maddy) to be?" I said mine had to be very intelligent. Marilyn said she didn't really want a husband, but if she had to have one he had to let her do whatever she wanted. Maddy began to dance around the room, his eyes closed, his arms holding an imaginary partner. "She's gotta be real cute," he said, "and she's gotta be a great daa-ancer." What he couldn't say then, at least partly because he wasn't yet sure himself, was that even more than a great dancer, she had to be a he.

"I ran into your mother a few months ago," my mother is saying. "She told me she never hears from you. What a bunch you all are!" I gaze at her in admiration. She hasn't laid eyes on Maddy Shapiro in more than twenty years, yet she feels perfectly free . . .

Maddy bursts out laughing and hugs her as people push past us, annoyed that we are blocking their mindless trek to the subway. "What a bunch *you* all are," he replies with something like affection in his voice. I look at him. I know that if Mrs. Shapiro was saying this his face would darken with anger and pain, but in *my* mother's mouth these sentences are *warmly* awful, *richly* exasperating. Out of such moments of detachment comes the narrative tale we tell of our lives.

"Nothing ever changes, does it." Maddy is shaking his head.

"Not true," my mother says shrewdly. "*You've* changed. I don't know what it is, but you're a completely different person."

"Not completely," Maddy retorts. "After all, you *did* recognize me, didn't you? Inside the brand-new Maddy you knew the old one was still there, and *you* spotted him. Couldn't fool *you*, could I?"

Well, well, Maddy.

One more question-and-answer routine and we've reached the limit of mutual interest. We exchange telephone numbers, promise to remain in touch, and part knowing we will not meet again.

60

My mother and I continue walking west on Twenty-third Street. She grasps my forearm between her fingers and leans toward me, confidentially. "Tell me something," she says. "Is Maddy what they call a homosexual?"

"Yes," I say.

"What do homosexuals do?" she asks.

"They do everything you do, Ma."

"What do you mean?"

"They fuck just like you do."

"How do they do that? Where?"

"In the ass."

"That must be painful."

"Sometimes it is. Mostly it's not."

"Do they get married?" she laughs.

"Some do. Most don't."

"Are they lonely?"

"As lonely as we are, Ma."

Now she is silent. She stares off into the middle distance in an odd, abstracted manner that has developed in her over the past year or so. She's alone inside that faraway look on her face, but this alone is different from the alone I'm very familiar with, the one that distorts her features into a mask of bitterness, the one in which she's counting up her grievances and disappointments. This alone is soft not bitter, full of interest, not a trace of self-pity in it. Now when her eyes narrow it is to take in more clearly what she knows, concentrate on what she has lived. She shakes herself as though from a penetrating dream.

"People have a right to their lives," she says quietly.

My father died at four o'clock in the morning on a day in late November. A telegram was delivered at five-thirty from the hospital where he had lain, terrified, for a week under an oxygen tent they said would save his life but I knew better. He had had three heart seizures in five days. The last one killed him. He was fifty-one years old. My mother was forty-six. My brother was nineteen. I was thirteen.

When the doorbell rang my brother was the first one out of bed, Mama right behind him, and me behind her. We all pushed into the tiny foyer. My brother stood in the doorway beneath the light from a sixty-watt bulb staring at a pale-yellow square of paper. My mother dug her nails into his arm. "Papa's dead, isn't he? Isn't he?" My brother slumped to the floor, and the screaming began.

"Oh," my mother screamed.

"Oh, my God," my mother screamed.

"Oh, my God, help me," my mother screamed.

The tears fell and rose and filled the hallway and ran into the kitchen and down across the living room and pushed against the walls of the two bedrooms and washed us all away.

Wailing women and frightened men surrounded my mother all that day and night. She clutched at her hair, and tore at her flesh, and fainted repeatedly. No one dared touch her. She was alone inside a circle of peculiar quar-

antine. They enclosed her but they did not intrude
had become magic. She was possessed.

With me they did as they pleased. Passing me among
themselves in an ecstasy of ritual pity, they isolated me
more thoroughly than actual neglect could have done. They
smothered me against their chests, choked me with indi-
gestible food, terrified my ears with a babble of numbing
reassurance. My only hope was retreat. I went unrespon-
sive, and I stayed that way.

Periodically, my mother's glazed eye would fasten on
me. She would then shriek my name and "An orphan!
Oh, God, you're an orphan!" No one had the courage to
remind her that according to Jewish custom you were an
orphan if your mother died, only half an orphan if your
father died. Perhaps it wasn't courage. Perhaps they understood that she didn't really mean me at all. She meant
herself. She was consumed by a sense of loss so primeval
she had taken all grief into her. Everyone's grief. That of
the wife, the mother, and the daughter. Grief had filled
her, and emptied her. She had become a vessel, a conduit, a manifestation. A remarkable fluidity, sensual and
demanding, was now hers. She'd be lying on the couch a
rag doll, her eyes dull, unseeing, tongue edging out of a
half-open mouth, arms hanging slack. Suddenly she'd jerk
straight up, body tense and alert, eyes sharp, forehead bathed
in sweat, a vein pulsing in her neck. Two minutes later
she was thrashing about, groveling against the couch, falling to the floor, skin chalky, eyes squeezed shut, mouth
tightly compressed. It went on for hours. For days. For
weeks, and for years.

I saw myself only as a prop in the extraordinary drama of Mama's bereavement. I didn't mind. I didn't know what I was supposed to be feeling, and I hadn't the time to find out. Actually I was frightened. I didn't object to being frightened. I supposed it as good a response as any other. Only, being frightened imposed certain responsibilities. For one, it demanded I not take my eyes off my mother for an instant. I never cried. Not once. I heard a woman murmur, "Unnatural child." I remember thinking, She doesn't understand. Papa's gone, and Mama obviously is going any minute now. If I cry I won't be able to see her. If I don't see her she's going to disappear. And then I'll be alone. Thus began my conscious obsession with keeping Mama in sight.

It began to snow in the middle of the first night Papa was in the ground. Twisting about on her sodden couch, my mother caught sight of the falling snow. "Oh, woe is me," she cried. "It's snowing on you, my beloved! You're all alone out there in the snow." A new calendar had begun marking time in the apartment: the first time it snowed on Papa's grave, the first time it rained, the first green of summer, the first gold of fall. Each first was announced in a high thin wail that to begin with acted like a needle on my heart, to end with a needle in my brain.

The funeral. Twenty years later when I was living as a journalist in the Middle East, I witnessed Arab funerals almost weekly—hundreds of men and women rushing through the streets, tearing at their clothes, uttering cries of an animal-like nature at a terrifying pitch of noise, people fainting, being trampled, while the crowd whirled screeching on. Westerners who might be standing beside

64

me in the street would shake their heads in amazement at a sight so foreign it confirmed them in their secret conviction that these people were indeed not like themselves. To me, however, it all seemed perfectly familiar, only a bit louder than I remembered, and the insanity parceled out quite a bit more. The way I remembered it, Mama had center stage at all times.

When I woke on the morning of the funeral she was tossing on the couch where she had lain forty-eight hours in clothes she refused to change out of, already crying. The crying was rhythmic, repetitious: it began in a low moan, quickly reached a pitch of shrillness, then receded in a loss of energy that recouped into the original moan. Each cycle was accomplished in a matter of two or three minutes and repeated without variation throughout that interminable morning, while eight or ten people (my brother and I, a few aunts and uncles, the neighbors) wandered aimlessly about the apartment: in and out of the kitchen, in and out of the living room, in and out of the bedrooms.

I remember no conversation; nor do I remember even a wordless embrace. True, explosive behavior was common among us while tender comfort was a difficulty, but it was Mama who had plunged us into muteness. Mama's suffering elevated Papa's death, made us all participants in an event of consequence, told us something had occurred we were not to support, not to live through, or at the very least be permanently stunted by. Still, it was Mama who occupied the dramatic center of the event while the rest of us shuffled about in the background, moving without tears or speech through a sludge of gray misery. It was as though we had all been absorbed into her spectacular abandonment, become witnesses to her loss rather than mourners ourselves. It was Mama who was on our minds as we roamed the gloomy apartment—who could think of Papa in the midst of such tumult?—Mama who must be watched and attended to, Mama whose mortal agony threatened general breakdown. Disaster seemed imminent rather than already accomplished.

At noon the house was suddenly spilling over with people who instead of going straight to the funeral parlor as they had been asked to showed up at the apartment. These people took us to the edge. As each new face placed itself directly within her view, my mother felt required to deliver up a fresh storm of tears and shrieks. My terror leaped. Now surely she would spin off into a hysteria from which there would be no return.

The time came to lift her from the couch, straighten her clothes, and get her out the door. No sooner were her legs over the side than she became spastic, began to twitch convulsively. Her eyeballs rolled up in her head, her body went limp, her feet refused to touch the floor, and she was dragged out the door like one headed for execution, carried along on a swarm of men and women crying, pleading, screaming, fainting in mimetic sympathy.

At the funeral parlor she tried to climb into the coffin. At the cemetery she tried to fling herself into the open grave. There were other moments at the funeral worthy of permanent record—my brother passed out, I looked so long into the casket I had to be pulled away, a political comrade announced at the grave that my father had been a wage slave in this America—but these moments are without clarity or sharpness of outline. They pall in memory beside the brilliant relentlessness of Mama's derangement.

The day of the funeral seemed to go on for ten days. There were never less than a dozen people wandering around the apartment. My mother lay on the couch weeping and fainting. One by one, each man and each woman in the apartment took a turn at her side, stared helplessly at her for a few minutes, assured her the worst that could happen had indeed happened, and then instructed her: This was *life*. There was nothing anyone could *do*. She had to gather herself *together*. And go *on*. That said, he or she would rise in relief and head for the kitchen, where there were always two to four women waiting to serve a cup of coffee, a bowl of soup, a plate of meat and vegetables. (I remember no cooking. Prepared food appeared magically every day.)

The kitchen was by far the most interesting place to be. Invariably, two of the women were my aunt Sarah and Mrs. Zimmerman, each of whom had less than a loving attachment to her own husband and certainly considered marriage an affliction. Both, however, had been silenced by my mother's awesome performance. Except every now and then irrepressible Mrs. Zimmerman, stirring her own soup at the stove, would mutter, "She lays there crying like a lunatic. If I would come home and find mine dead, it would be a blessing." Sarah would remain silent but someone else in the kitchen, another aunt, a cousin, a friend (why did it always seem to be a woman in a black hat with a dotted veil?), would reprimand Mrs. Zimmerman. "Please, missus!" she'd say. "*She* is not *you*. And a

67

little respect for the dead, if you don't mind." Mrs. Zimmerman would flush deeply and open her mouth wide, but before a sound came out Sarah would lay a hand on her arm and beg that there not be a scene. I'd be at the table, sitting on the wooden bench, often in the crook of Nettie's arm. Animated by the exchange, I'd be disappointed by Sarah's interference. Then Nettie's head would drop, and I'd feel her mouth smiling into my hair. It was as good as if Mrs. Zimmerman had spoken. And shortly, Mrs. Zimmerman did speak. And another tart response cut the air.

I didn't know that not every woman who had lost a husband would be carrying on like Mama, but I did know that the conversation in the kitchen was immensely interesting. One spoke sharply, another speculatively, a third imperiously. The talk was hard and bright, gave the room charge and intensity. Nettie, of course, hardly spoke at all but her body, often in close contact with mine, spoke for her, its speech hidden, restless, amused. I couldn't figure out what was going on in the kitchen, but the responsiveness among the women told me this was a live issue. And the way they dived in! I loved it. Felt nourished and protected, delighted and relieved by it. I remember, especially, the relief.

There was no softness anywhere, not in the kitchen or in the living room, no bland or soothing element on which to heal yourself, or even rub a wound. Still, the difference between the living room and the kitchen was the difference between suffocation and survival. The living room was all monotonous dread, congealed and airless. Here you took a deep breath, held it until you were smothering, then either got out or went under. In the kitchen there was pitch and tone, the atmosphere fell and rose, dwindled away, churned itself up again. There was movement and space, light and air. You could breathe. You could live.

Nettie was around much of the time. Around me, not Mama. She hovered in the doorway or the foyer, sat down shyly in the kitchen, but rarely did she enter the living room. All those respectable Jewish women: she couldn't make her way past them to Mama. Once in a while she'd cross the threshold and stand there like a child, twisting her hands behind her back. My mother would have to spot her, stretch out her arm and wail, "Nettie! I've lost my beloved!" before Nettie felt free (that is, commanded) to rush over, fall to her knees beside the couch, and burst into tears herself.

With me, however, she felt not only free but equal and necessary. She sat with me on the kitchen bench, her arm slung around my neck in an easy embrace, combing my hair with her long fingers. We both knew she had neither the wisdom nor the authority to ease my anxiety (she wasn't even a confidante, she'd always talked more easily to me than I to her), but she could become another orphan, snuggle down companionably with me as she had with Richie, give me the consolation of her warm, helpless body.

Something else began to happen during those funeral-week hours we shared on the kitchen bench. When the women talked about men and marriage, and I felt Nettie's secret smile in my hair and she stifling her laughter against my back, a disturbing excitement ran through me. She

69

knew something no one else in the room knew, and I could feel her wanting to pull me into her knowledge, have me join her there, become her true friend.

The invitation lay in the movement of her body against mine, its freedom and its intimacy. Her motions were rhythmic, her embrace reassuring. She stroked my hair and my shoulder. I felt soothed and sedated. I leaned into her. Her touch began to seem insistent. I felt myself being pulled. Toward what I didn't know. It was as though Nettie stood at the mouth of something dark and soft, drawing me on, her body saying to me: Come. Don't be afraid. I'll pull you through. A dreamy, spreading blur dissolved in my head, my chest. I drowsed against her: open willing aroused.

Suddenly terror prickled on my skin. I felt myself pitching forward, headfirst. The soft dark place was a black void. And she? Who was she? Just a secret-smiling girl-woman, a big kid herself. When we traded fantasies I always felt older. If I went into the dark with her we'd be two kids in there, alone together. How could I trust her? She was no one to trust. My body stiffened in her embrace. She started up, as lost in the hypnotic moment as I, bewildered and alarmed by the suddenness of my withdrawal.

"I want to go see Mama," I said.

Easy as a cat, Nettie's eyes went opaque, her neck grew long, she rearranged her arms and legs. I was free to leave the table.

In the living room I sank to the floor beside my mother, who immediately pressed my head into her breasts. Her strong arms held me, her moans convulsed me. In a matter of seconds the power of Nettie's drowsy allure had been dissipated. I shivered inside myself as though I had made a narrow escape. My anxiety felt cold and scummy. I let Mama crush me against her hot chest. I did not resist. Mama was where I belonged. With Mama the issue was clear: I had trouble breathing but I was safe.

It rained earlier in the day and now, at one in the afternoon, for a minute and a half, New York is washed clean. The streets glitter in the pale spring sunlight. Cars radiate dust-free happiness. Storefront windows sparkle mindlessly. Even people look made anew.

We're walking down Eighth Avenue into the Village. At the corner of Eighth and Greenwich is a White Tower hamburger joint, where a group of derelicts in permanent residence entertain visiting out-of-towners from Fourteenth Street, Chelsea, even the Bowery. This afternoon the party on the corner, often raucous, is definitely on the gloomy side, untouched by weather renewal. As we pass the restaurant doors, however, one gentleman detaches from the group, takes two or three uncertain steps, and bars our way. He stands, swaying, before us. He is black, somewhere between twenty-five and sixty. His face is cut and swollen, the eyelids three-quarters shut. His hair is a hundred filthy matted little pigtails, his pants are held up by a piece of rope, his shoes are two sizes too large, the feet inside them bare. So is his chest, visible beneath a grimy tweed coat that swings open whenever he moves. This creature confronts us, puts out his hand palm up, and speaks.

"Can you ladies let me have a thousand dollars for a martini?" he inquires.

My mother looks directly into his face. "I know we're in an inflation," she says, "but a thousand dollars for a martini?"

His mouth drops. It's the first time in God knows how long that a mark has acknowledged his existence. "You're beautiful," he burbles at her. "Beautiful."

"Look on him," she says to me in Yiddish. "Just look on him."

He turns his bleary eyelids in my direction. "Whad-she-say?" he demands. "Whad-she-say?"

"She said you're breaking her heart," I tell him.

"She-say-that?" His eyes nearly open. "She-say-that?"

I nod. He whirls at her. "Take me home and make love to me," he croons, and right there in the street, in the middle of the day, he begins to bay at the moon. "I need you," he howls at my mother and doubles over, his fist in his stomach. "I need you."

She nods at him. "I need too," she says dryly. "Fortunately or unfortunately, it is not you I need." And she propels me around the now motionless derelict. Paralyzed by recognition, he will no longer bar our progress down the street.

We cross Abingdon Square and walk into Bleecker Street. The gentrified West Village closes around us, makes us not peaceful but quiet. We walk through block after block of antique stores, gourmet shops, boutiques, not speaking. But for how long can my mother and I not speak?

"So I'm reading the biography you gave me," she says. I look at her, puzzled, and then I remember. "Oh!" I smile in wide delight. "Are you enjoying it?"

"Listen," she begins. The smile drops off my face and my stomach contracts. That "listen" means she is about to trash the book I gave her to read. She is going to say, "What. What's here? What's here that I don't already know? I *lived* through it. I know it all. What can this writer tell me that I don't already know? Nothing. To *you* it's interesting, but to me? How can this be interesting to me?"

On and on she'll go, the way she does when she thinks she doesn't understand something and she's scared, and she's taking refuge in scorn and hypercriticality.

The book I gave her to read is a biography of Josephine Herbst, a thirties writer, a stubborn willful raging woman grabbing at politics and love and writing, in there punching until the last minute.

"Listen," my mother says now in the patronizing tone she thinks conciliatory. "Maybe this is interesting to you, but not to me. I lived through all this. I know it all. What can I learn from this? Nothing. To you it's interesting. Not to me."

Invariably, when she speaks so, my head fills with blood and before the sentences have stopped pouring from her mouth I am lashing out at her. "You're an ignoramus, you know nothing, only a know-nothing talks the way you do. The point of having lived through it, as you say, is only that the background is familiar, so the book is made richer, not that you could have written the book. People a thousand times more educated than you have read and learned from this book, but *you* can't learn from it?" On and on I would go, thoroughly ruining the afternoon for both of us.

However, in the past year an odd circumstance has begun to obtain. On occasion, my head fails to fill with blood. I become irritated but remain calm. Not falling into a rage, I do not make a holocaust of the afternoon. Today, it appears, one of those moments is upon us. I turn to my mother, throw my left arm around her still solid back, place my right hand on her upper arm, and say, "Ma, if this book is not interesting to you, that's fine. You can say that." She looks coyly at me, eyes large, head half-turned; *now* she's interested. "But don't say it has nothing to teach you. That there's nothing here. That's unworthy of you, and of the book, and of me. You demean us all when you say that." Listen to me. Such wisdom. And all of it gained ten minutes ago.

Silence. Long silence. We walk another block. Silence. She's looking off into that middle distance. I take my lead from her, matching my steps to hers. I do not speak, do not press her. Another silent block.

"That Josephine Herbst," my mother says. "She certainly carried on, didn't she?"

Relieved and happy, I hug her. "She didn't know what she was doing either, Ma, but yes, she carried on."

"I'm jealous," my mother blurts at me. "I'm jealous she lived her life, I didn't live mine."

Mama went to work five weeks after my father died. He had left us two thousand dollars. To work or not to work was not a debatable question. But it's hard to imagine what would have happened if economic necessity had not forced her out of the house. As it was, it seemed to me that she lay on a couch in a half-darkened room for twenty-five years with her hand across her forehead murmuring, "I can't." Even though she could, and did.

She pulled on her girdle and her old gray suit, stepped into her black suede chunky heels, applied powder and lipstick to her face, and took the subway downtown to an employment agency where she got a job clerking in an office for twenty-eight dollars a week. After that, she rose each morning, got dressed and drank coffee, made out a grocery list for me, left it together with money on the kitchen table, walked four blocks to the subway station, bought the *Times*, read it on the train, got off at Forty-second Street, entered her office building, sat down at her desk, put in a day's work, made the trip home at five o'clock, came in the apartment door, slumped onto the kitchen bench for supper, then onto the couch where she instantly sank into a depression she welcomed like a warm bath. It was as though she had worked all day to earn the despair waiting faithfully for her at the end of her unwilling journey into daily life.

Weekends, of course, the depression was unremitting.

A black and wordless pall hung over the apartment all of Saturday and all of Sunday. Mama neither cooked, cleaned, nor shopped. She took no part in idle chatter: the exchange of banalities that fills a room with human presence, declares an interest in being alive. She would not laugh, respond, or participate in any of the compulsive kitchen talk that went on among the rest of us: me, my aunt Sarah, Nettie, my brother. She spoke minimally, and when she did speak her voice was uniformly tight and miserable, always pulling her listener back to a proper recollection of her "condition." If she answered the phone her voice dropped a full octave when she said hello; she could not trust that the caller would otherwise gauge properly the abiding nature of her pain. For five years she did not go to a movie, a concert, a public meeting. She worked, and she suffered.

Widowhood provided Mama with a higher form of being. In refusing to recover from my father's death she had discovered that her life was endowed with a seriousness her years in the kitchen had denied her. She remained devoted to this seriousness for thirty years. She never tired of it, never grew bored or restless in its company, found new ways to keep alive the interest it deserved and had so undeniably earned.

Mourning Papa became her profession, her identity, her persona. Years later, when I was thinking about the piece of politics inside of which we had all lived (Marxism and the Communist Party), and I realized that people who worked as plumbers, bakers, or sewing-machine operators had thought of themselves as thinkers, poets, and scholars

76

because they were members of the Communist Party, I saw that Mama had assumed her widowhood in much the same way. It elevated her in her own eyes, made of her a spiritually significant person, lent richness to her gloom and rhetoric to her speech. Papa's death became a religion that provided ceremony and doctrine. A woman-who-has-lost-the-love-of-her-life was now her orthodoxy: she paid it Talmudic attention.

Papa had never been so real to me in life as he was in death. Always a somewhat shadowy figure, benign and smiling, standing there behind Mama's dramatics about married love, he became and remained what felt like the necessary instrument of her permanent devastation. It was almost as though she had lived with Papa in order that she might arrive at this moment. Her distress was so all-consuming it seemed ordained. For me, surely, it ordered the world anew.

The air I breathed was soaked in her desperation, made thick and heady by it, exciting and dangerous. Her pain became my element, the country in which I lived, the rule beneath which I bowed. It commanded me, made me respond against my will. I longed endlessly to get away from her, but I could not leave the room when she was in it. I dreaded her return from work, but I was never not there when she came home. In her presence anxiety swelled my lungs (I suffered constrictions of the chest and sometimes felt an iron ring clamped across my skull), but I locked myself in the bathroom and wept buckets on her behalf. On Friday I prepared myself for two solid days of weeping and sighing and the mysterious reproof that depression leaks into the air like the steady escape of gas when the pilot light is extinguished. I woke up guilty and went to bed guilty, and on weekends the guilt accumulated into low-grade infection.

She made me sleep with her for a year, and for twenty years afterward I could not bear a woman's hand on me. Afraid to sleep alone, she slung an arm across my stomach, pulled me toward her, fingered my flesh nervously, inattentively. I shrank from her touch: she never noticed. I yearned toward the wall, couldn't get close enough, was always being pulled back. My body became a column of aching stiffness. I must have been excited. Certainly I was repelled.

For two years she dragged me to the cemetery every second or third Sunday morning. The cemetery was in Queens. This meant taking three buses and traveling an hour and fifteen minutes each way. When we climbed onto the third bus she'd begin to cry. Helplessly, I would embrace her. Her cries would grow louder. Inflamed with discomfort, my arm would stiffen around her shoulder and I would stare at the black rubber floor. The bus would arrive at the last stop just as she reached the verge of convulsion.

"We have to get off, Ma," I'd plead in a whisper.

She would shake herself reluctantly (she hated to lose momentum once she'd started on a real wail) and slowly climb down off the bus. As we went through the gates of the cemetery, however, she'd rally to her own cause. She would clutch my arm and pull me across miles of tombstones (neither of us ever seemed to remember the exact location of the grave), stumbling like a drunk, lurching

78

about and shrieking: "Where's Papa? Help me find Papa! They've lost Papa. Beloved! I'm coming. Wait, only wait, I'm coming!" Then we would find the grave and she would fling herself across it, arrived at last in a storm of climactic release. On the way home she was a rag doll. And I? Numb and dumb, only grateful to have survived the terror of the earlier hours.

One night when I was fifteen I dreamed that the entire apartment was empty, stripped of furniture and brilliantly whitewashed, the rooms gleaming with sun and the whiteness of the walls. A long rope extended the length of the apartment, winding at waist-level through all the rooms. I followed the rope from my room to the front door. There in the open doorway stood my dead father, gray-faced, surrounded by mist and darkness, the rope tied around the middle of his body. I laid my hands on the rope and began to pull, but try as I might I could not lift him across the threshold. Suddenly my mother appeared. She laid her hands over mine and began to pull also. I tried to shake her off, enraged at her interference, but she would not desist, and I did so want to pull him in I said to myself, "All right, I'll even let her have him, if we can just get him inside."

For years I thought the dream needed no interpretation, but now I think I longed to get my father across the threshold not out of guilt and sexual competition but so that I could get free of Mama. My skin crawled with her. She was everywhere, all over me, inside and out. Her influence clung, membrane-like, to my nostrils, my eyelids, my open mouth. I drew her into me with every breath I

79

took. I drowsed in her etherizing atmosphere, could not escape the rich and claustrophobic character of her presence, her being, her suffocating suffering femaleness.

I didn't know the half of it.

One afternoon, in the year of the dream, I was sitting with Nettie. She was making lace, and I was drinking tea. She began to dream out loud. "I think you'll meet a really nice boy this year," she said. "Someone older than yourself. Almost out of college. Ready to get a good job. He'll fall in love with you, and soon you'll be married."

"That's ridiculous," I said sharply.

Nettie let her hands, with the lace still in them, fall to her lap. "You sound just like your mother," she said softly.

That's ridiculous. Sometimes I think I was born saying, "That's ridiculous." It shoots out of me as easily as good-morning-good-evening-have-a-nice-day-take-care. It is my most on-automatic response. The variety of observations that allows "That's ridiculous" to pass from my brain to my tongue is astonishing.

"Adultery makes modern marriage work," someone will say.

"That's ridiculous," I'll say.

"Edgar Allan Poe is the most underrated writer in American literature," someone will say.

"That's ridiculous," I'll say.

"Sports have an influence on people's values."

"That's ridiculous."

"Movies have an influence on people's fantasies."

"That's ridiculous."

80

"If I could take a year off from work my life would be changed."

"That's ridiculous."

"Did you know that most women refuse to leave the husbands who beat them?"

"That's ridiculous!"

Three years ago I ran into Dorothy Levinson on the street. We hugged and kissed many times. She stood there repeating my name. Then she smiled and said, "Do you still say, 'That's ridiculous'?" I stared at her. She hadn't seen me since I was thirteen years old. I felt the blood beating in my cheeks. Yes, I nodded, I do. She threw back her head and nearly had a heart attack laughing. On the spot she invited me to have dinner in a restaurant that night with her and her husband. What an evening that was.

Dorothy Levinson. So beautiful it twisted your heart. Now here she was, fifty, slim, lovely, full of shrewd Jewish wit and crinkle-eyed affection, her face looking remarkably as her mother's had at this same age: soft and kindly, slightly puzzled, slightly sad.

The Levinsons. I had loved them all—Dorothy, the four boys, the mad parents—but most of all I had loved Davey, the youngest boy, when we were both twelve, and how I had suffered because he hadn't loved me at all. There he'd been, thin and athletic, with a headful of glossy black curls and brilliant black eyes (every little girl had wanted him), and there I'd been, pudgy, sullen, superior. The whole thing had been quite hopeless.

The Levinsons were our summer people. Between my tenth and my thirteenth summers we were in residence at

81

Ben's Bungalows in the Catskill Mountains. Two contingents dominated this bungalow colony: people like ourselves from the Bronx and people like the Levinsons from the Lower East Side. Or, as my mother put it, "the politically enlightened and the Jewish gangsters."

The Jewish gangsters had it all over the politically enlightened in the mountains. They learned quickly where good times in the country were to be had, and went after them as single-mindedly as they pursued their share of the action on Grand Street. They swam out farther in the lake than we did, roamed farther afield in search of wild fruit, trekked deeper into the forest. They danced in electric rainstorms, slept on the open mountainside on hot nights, persisted in losing their virginity wherever possible, and in making everyone else lose theirs as well.

The darkest and wildest of them all were the Levinsons—from Sonny the oldest son, to Dorothy the only daughter, down to my beloved Davey. They were so beautiful it was hard to look directly at them. Two summers in a row we shared a double bungalow with the Levinsons, and I was in a continual state as they slammed in and out of the screen door that hung on the same thin frame as ours. I remember those summers as flashes of black silky curls whirling by in the noonday sun, or quick darting glances in the bright shade from a pair of black eyes filled with scheming laughter. They were always going somewhere, planning something. Whatever they did it was the thing to do. Wherever they went it was the place to go. I longed to be asked to join them, but I never was. I stayed behind in the bungalow with my mother or read on the grass nearby, while they ran out into an intensity of sweet

summer air to catch salamanders and frogs, explore abandoned houses, plunge repeatedly into the lake, feel sun
burning into bare brown flesh, long after I had been called
in to supper.

Dorothy and her husband and I went to a restaurant in
the Village, and the talk plunged headlong into the past.
Dorothy's husband, an accountant, knew he didn't have a
chance and settled good-naturedly into playing audience
for the evening. Dorothy and I, absorbed by every scrap of
memory—Grand Street, the Bronx, Ben's Bungalows—
talked over each other's voices, shrieking with laughter at
everything, at nothing.

Dorothy kept asking if I remembered. Remember the
abandoned house in the forest? Remember the berry-picking
on the high hills far away? And the scratched asses from
lying on the thorns to neck? Remember the warmth and
vulgarity of the women on the porch on Sunday night?
Dorothy's memories were richly detailed, my own sketchy.
It wasn't just that she was eight years older. She was a
Levinson. She had lived it more fully than I had.

Meanwhile, I kept asking, How's Sonny? How're Larry
and Miltie? And your father. How is he? (I didn't ask for
Mrs. Levinson, because she was dead, and I didn't ask for
Davey, now a rabbi in Jerusalem, because I didn't want to
know.)

"Sonny?" Dorothy said. "All we do is analyze. Analyze,
analyze. When Sonny was in the army Mama got sick.
Papa had run out on her. Sonny came home. He got down
on his knees beside the bed and he said, 'I'll take care of
you, Ma.' She said, 'I want Jake.' Sonny walked out of the
apartment. Later he said, 'When I realized she loved him

more than she loved me I said to myself, Fuck her.' But he never got over it. He's got a nice wife, good kids, lives near me. You know we all still live downtown, don't you? Sure you know. So now Sonny comes in the apartment, a friend is sitting on the couch, he looks the situation over, jerks his head in the direction of the bedroom, says, I gotta talk to you; my friend starts laughing. But that's it. We don't really share anything. He comes over, gets analyzed, goes home. Larry? He's 240 pounds now. Got a girlfriend, but he still lives in the old apartment on Essex Street, she shouldn't think he's getting involved, he's only been with her six years. Davey! Don't you want to know how Davey is? Davey's wonderful! Who would have thought my baby brother would turn out spiritual? But he has. He's *spiritual*."

I nearly said, "That's ridiculous." Stopped just in time. But I couldn't let it go, all the same. Silent throughout the recital on Sonny and Larry, now I felt I had to speak. "Oh, Dorothy," I said, very gently I thought, "Davey's not spiritual."

Dorothy's eyes dropped to the table, her brows drew together. When she looked up again her eyes were very bright, her mouth shaped in an uncertain smile.

"What do you mean?" she asked.

"If Davey had left Essex Street at eighteen he wouldn't be spiritual today," I said. "He's looking for a way to put his life together, and he's got no equipment with which to do it. So he turned religious. It's a mark of how lost he is, not how found he is, that he's a rabbi in Jerusalem."

Dorothy nodded and nodded at me. Her voice when she spoke was unnaturally quiet. "I guess that's one way you

84

could look at it," she said. I laughed and shrugged. We dropped it.

On we went, falling back repeatedly to stories of the bungalow colony. Dorothy did most of the talking. As the hours passed Dorothy did all the talking. She talked faster and faster, the sentences tumbling one after another. A mosaic of emotional memory began to emerge: how she had seen me, how she had seen my mother, how she had seen my mother in relation to her mother. I began to feel uncomfortable. She remembered it all so vividly. She had been so intent on us. Especially on my mother.

She laughed heartily as she spoke, a strong rocking laughter. Suddenly she turned full face to me and said, "You never really enjoyed it like we did. You were always so critical. For such a little kid you were amazing. It's like you knew you were more intelligent than anyone else around, and you were always seeing how silly or pointless or ridiculous—your favorite word—everything was. Your mother, also, was so much better than anyone else around. And she was, she was. Your father adored her. She used to walk beside him, his arm around her and she holding on to him, God, did she hold on to him, holding on for dear life, clinging like to a life raft, and looking around to make sure everyone saw how happy she was with her lover-like husband. It was as though she wanted to make every woman there jealous. And *my* mother? My father came up once during the whole summer. She used to cry over your mother: 'Look how good he is to her, and look how Jake treats me. She's got everything, I've got nothing.' "

Dorothy laughed again: as though she was afraid to speak without laughing. "My mother was kind," she said. "She had a kind heart. Your mother? She was *organized*. My mother would sit up with her own kids when they were sick, and she'd sit up with you, too. Your mother would march into the kitchen like a top sergeant and say to my mother, 'Levinson, stop crying, put on a brassiere, fix yourself up.' "

More laughter, by now the taste of iron in it. Dorothy struggled with herself to stop, to get off my mother and her mother. Abruptly she took her memories back to a time before my time, and began to tell us of the Jewish mystics traveling around on the bungalow-colony circuit when she was eight or ten years old. "All the women would sit around in a circle in the dark," she said, "with a candle on the table. The medium would close her eyes, tremble, and say, '*Habe sich, tischele.*' Lift yourself, little table." ("And would it?" "Of course!") "Women would start to scream and faint. 'Is that you, Moishe? *Oy gevalt!* it's Moishe!' More screaming, more fainting."

Dorothy threw me a sharp look and said, "Your mother would have marched in, turned on the light, and said, 'What is this nonsense?' " Dorothy's husband and I both stared open-mouthed at her. Before he could stop her she leaned toward me and hissed, "She never loved you. She never loved anybody."

The next morning I realized that although I had not said "That's ridiculous" before I scored off Davey, Dorothy had nonetheless heard the words. The mother in her had heard the mother in me.

I saw the man again today. This time it had been five years. My mother and I were on upper Broadway, looking for a shoe store recommended for its walking shoes. As we approached Eighty-third Street he turned the corner. Involuntarily I flinched. "What is it?" my mother asked. "Nothing," I said. But her eyes had followed mine and she saw that I was held by the face of a man like that of fifty other derelict-looking men one might pass in a twenty-minute walk on Broadway.

"Who is that?" she pressed me. "You know him?"

"Remember the man in the doorway years ago? The one I see every now and then?"

"Yes, of course. That's him?"

I nodded.

She turned her bold urban stare directly on him.

It happened twelve years ago. I was living on First Avenue at Twentieth Street in two whitewashed rooms flooded with eastern light, and a tree outside that filled the window in spring and summer with birds and foliage. Across the avenue Stuyvesant Town, one of the oldest middle-income housing projects in the city. On my side of the avenue Irish and Italian tenements where people had been born, raised, married, and raised families of their own in the same apartments. Binding us all together, the glittery noise and movement of First Avenue. When my aunt Sarah first came to visit she leaned out the window, breathed in the

87

fumes, and said, "Just what I love. Rush, rush!" I felt the same. I deeply loved First Avenue. Loved it and felt safe on it. People sat in windows watching the neighbors all day long. Shopkeepers registered every foreign and familiar face moving past their storefronts. The equation was simple: you lost anonymity, you gained protection.

One Saturday morning in June I ran down to the supermarket a block away to get a container of milk. The avenue sparkled in the early sun. The air was sweet, balmy, pollinated. Coming back from the market I suffered an allergic attack of "spring fever." I sneezed so hard I couldn't move: stood helpless on the street, holding myself against the rapid-fire seizure that had taken hold of my body. As the fit drew to an end, only one more sneeze in me, I could feel it, my head lifted in expectation of deliverance. At that moment my eyes locked with the eyes of a man coming toward me in the morning crowd. He was slim and Mediterranean-dark, in his forties, wearing a white shirt and black pants, carrying a brown paper lunch bag. A waiter, I thought, on his way to work. As the final sneeze was expelled my neck and shoulders lifted reflexively and I laughed, into his eyes, as it happened. Clearly, I was laughing at myself. No other interpretation of the gesture was remotely possible. The man didn't even smile back. His eyes flicked on me, off me. He kept going, I kept going.

I crossed the street and turned into the doorway of my little building. As I was about to insert the key in the vestibule door I felt a hand on my shoulder. I turned. The man in the white shirt and black pants was standing there, blocking me in. His eyes were pinpoints of rage. His mouth was twisted to the side, the lips white with strain. His neck was pulsing. "You tired of livin'?" he said to me.

Omigod, I thought.

"What do you mean?" I asked politely.

"You were laughin' back there. Ya tired of livin', aincha?"

"Oh, you misunderstood," I purred shamelessly. "I was laughing at myself. I've got sneezing fits. I was laughing because I was sneezing so hard I couldn't move. I wasn't laughing at you. Did you think I was laughing at you? Oh no!"

He heard nothing I said. His face remained closed against me. If anything, the pinpoints of rage glowed harder. He looked at the keys in my hand. "You live here?" he said. His hand made an upward motion. "Come on," he said. "Upstairs."

"No," I babbled. "I don't live here. I'm just visiting."

"Upstairs," he said. "Come on, upstairs."

"I don't live here. We can't go upstairs."

In a motion of strength derived from terror I placed my open hand against his chest and pushed. He lost his balance and toppled backward into the street. I jerked past him into the crowd and ran. Ran to the end of the block, then into the next block, and into the supermarket. I stood there, just beyond the checkout counters, breathing hard. I didn't know what to do, where to go, whom to speak to. Without warning, the familiar had passed into nightmare.

I wandered around the market for thirty minutes, then made a break for it, walking fast, head down, away from my building, somehow the container of milk no longer in my hand. Hours later, thoroughly exhausted, I returned to *not to Moms?*

First Avenue and darted unmolested through my own doorway, not leaving the apartment for the rest of that day and evening.

Three years later I saw the man in the white shirt and the black pants on East Fourteenth Street. It was late fall. He was wearing a thin leather jacket and hugging a brown paper parcel to his chest. I backed quickly into a doorway, out of the line of his vision. He looked exactly as he had three years before, but as he drew closer I saw that he stumbled when he walked, and his eyes were horribly anxious.

Four years after that I saw him again, on West Eighth Street. His hair was heavily streaked with gray now, his skin yellow, his chin covered with white stubble. As he came abreast of me I stepped out of the doorway I had ducked into. He looked at me, through me. His gaze, as I had suspected, was fixed, unseeing.

Now, five years later, here he was on Broadway, his hair iron-gray, his stare wild, his walk unsteady, his hands flailing at the air. His clothes were out of the men's shelter, and his face so ill-looking you wanted to put him in a hospital for a month before we even discussed the situation.

My mother looked curiously at me. "Why were you afraid of *him?*" she asked. "You could knock him over with one hand."

"Ma, he didn't look like that twelve years ago. Believe me."

She continued to stare after him as he shambled down Broadway, bumping into people left and right.

90

"You're growing old together," she said to me. "You and what frightens you."

I'm fourteen years old. It's an evening in late spring. I push open the door of Nettie's apartment. The kitchen is steeped in a kind of violet gloom, soft, full, intense. The room is empty: bathed in the lovely half-light, but empty. I stop short. The door wasn't locked, someone must be home. I walk through to the inner room. I stop on the threshold. The light is even weaker here. My eyes adjust. I see Nettie and the priest lying across the paisley-covered bed. She is naked, he is dressed. He is flat on his back. She lies half across him. His body is rigid, hers is spilling over. I can see her smiling in the half-dark. She moves across him like a cat, and like a cat watches closely even as she purrs. She arches her back and lifts herself, only to fall again toward him. Her breast drops into his nerveless hand. Vibrancy flows through me like electric shock. I can feel them both. Inside me. I feel her, and I feel him. I am the breast, and I am the hand. I am her pleasure, I am his pain. I shiver. The shiver becomes a tremble, the tremble a shudder. The shudder brings me abruptly into contact with something close by. I look down. There beside me is Richie, five years old, strapped into a chair, staring at the scene on the bed. I retreat, moving back face forward to the front door.

The next morning Nettie sits in a flowered housedress at her kitchen table, mending a skirt, her face lowered, smiling to herself. She looks up at me, her green eyes falsely innocent. "Did you come in here last night?" she asks. We are all her defeated enemies this morning. Calmly I think: She hates men.

When did it begin? When did she start roaming the streets? Or sitting in the boat park? When did she first bring home the priest? Or a man from the park? When did the chicken-store owner who looked like Joseph Stalin appear at the door early in the morning? When did Whitey, the only serious delinquent on the block, first come up to the apartment? Mama said a year after Rick's death. "For one year she was good," she used to say. "And then she went to town."

When did I begin to take it in? And what did I make of it? When was the first I *knew* something about her in a world where men were sex, but women?—weren't we just supposed to get out of the way when we saw it coming?

Marilyn Kerner and I were riding our bikes in Bronx Park after school one day late in May. This was our daily practice from early spring until late fall. We would enter the park two blocks from our house, near the entrance to the zoo, and start riding. Sometimes we'd ride hard and fast straight through to Bronx Park East, a good hour from home. Sometimes we'd ride to special places, some particular clump of rock and bush we had made our own. Sometimes we'd circle around just inside the park, talking, more interested in the conversation than the ride, but still in comforting motion on the bike. With the bikes under us we felt free and brave: intelligent explorers in a foreign land. The street, I knew, was mine—the street was human exchange, people smarts, on the street I held my own— but the park? Henri Rousseau's paintings remind me of the way I felt about the park. I would glimpse the wild and the primeval in a landscaped piece of world carefully re-made to resemble the original tangle, and there I'd be, flat against it, a little Jewish girl on a bike unable to imagine herself other than talking.

Even so, we'd ride hard on those spring afternoons, the wind and stir we created matching the one just beginning inside ourselves, the light and speed irradiating, the ride an extraordinary rush, delicious and frightening, a burst of startled sensation.

Across the road from the zoo the Bronx River had been dammed up and a small lake and waterfall created. On the lake were boats, rented by the hour out of a boathouse built at the end closest to the waterfall. The boathouse was gaily decorated and sat, at the edge of the lake, on a cir-cular concrete patio that had been laid down by the Parks Service, with benches in tiers placed in a half circle at the edge of the patio. These benches were painted bright green each spring. From certain angles on the benches the lake looked as though it went on forever. I had been out on the lake a hundred times, I knew every curve of its outline, knew exactly how confined it was, and yet each time I sat on the benches I dreamed out at the water and imagined that just around the bend, out of sight, the lake suddenly lengthened into a mysterious channel and entered a place I'd never been before. I thought everyone who sat on the benches looking out at the water had similar thoughts, that the benches were filled with dreamers, that people came there to dream.

There was a ride Marilyn and I took that ended at the benches. The ride was brief but so complicated it seemed a long day's journey, and on short afternoons we took it so as not to feel cheated of time on the bike. You'd take a path on the far side of the waterfall that climbed a rocky stretch of ground high above the river, twisting and turning away into thick, tangled underbrush, bending back across the woods, cutting through a hill of black rock flat and sinuous at the top, then curving swiftly around and down toward the lake, rushing heedlessly toward the boathouse through a stretch of high open meadow and tall grasses, the whole world under an empty sky and the wind in your lungs an excitement from which you would never recover, braking hard just as you were about to come crashing into the concrete patio. Joy. The whole ride was pure joy.

On this afternoon in May Marilyn and I came riding down through the meadow, and just as we were braking I saw Nettie sitting on a bench on the lowest tier closest to the water. Not far from her sat a man I had never seen before. They seemed to know each other, and yet not know each other. The man was sitting with his arms extended across the back of the bench, his legs stretched out before him. He had a brown felt hat tilted forward on his head and a toothpick in his mouth. His face was not turned directly toward Nettie but, rather, angled at her. Nettie, too, seemed to be sitting peculiarly. The upper half of her body faced directly toward the lake but the lower half was twisted toward the man, her long midriff made even longer by her position. She was wearing a thin summer dress, although it was only mid-spring. Her red hair tumbled about her shoulders. Her legs were bare and on her feet a pair of high-heeled scuffs. She swung one leg back and forth, the scuff falling away from the heel each time her leg went out. I knew even before the bike had come to a halt that the two of them, sitting as they were, angled toward each other but not facing each other, said something. The posture was a kind of speech. I couldn't read the message, but it slapped hard against the light in my eyes, the joy in my chest, the charge running through my arms and legs.

Marilyn had also spotted Nettie and the man. Without consultation we halted our bikes far enough from the benches so that Nettie couldn't see us, and sat leaning forward over our handlebars. For a moment neither of us spoke, we simply watched.

"She's picking him up," Marilyn said softly.

"What do you mean?" I asked.

"That's a strange man, and she's picking him up."

"How do you know that?"

"Can't you see? By the way they're sitting? And besides, that's what people do here."

"You're kidding. How do you know that?"

"*Every*one knows that."

"Are you *sure*?"

"I'm sure."

So the people who sat here late in the day in spring and summer were not dreaming about unexpected channels of water just beyond view, they were determining on human adventure right there on the bench beside them. I stared at Marilyn, but I believed her. She knew more about these things than I did.

Where, I always wondered afterward, had Richie been that afternoon? Mama said that in fact Richie was with Nettie most of the time, he provided her with interest value and legitimacy. Not to mention that she had nowhere to leave him or anyone to leave him with. I wondered how Mama knew this, as Nettie never discussed her forays into the street with any of us. We deduced activity from consequence. Men would be seen entering or leaving the apartment. Some came once and never again, some came three or four times, some came for weeks or months. I don't think she took money from them. She may have let them give her things (a winter coat, a bag of groceries, a trip to the ocean), but it wasn't money she was after.

She brought them home from foreign parts: walks in adjacent neighborhoods, subway trips she made downtown. The priest came from downtown. She had determined after her marriage to Rick never to enter a church again and she was raising Richie to know he was Jewish, but in her loneliness she was drawn repeatedly to the oldest comfort of her life. She took seriously her lapse from the Church, did not think it her right to approach the altar, sink to her knees, or ask for communion, but she would search out churches of all kinds just to sit in the back and feel brief respite in a looming candlelit interior while Richie played with the buttons on her dress, mesmerized by her heaving breast as she sighed and trembled and wept a little.

One day she was wandering around the department stores

96

on Thirty-fourth Street. She passed a church near Gimbel's. On impulse she walked in and slipped into a confessional. The priest was young and must have been easily moved by her broken murmurs, her whispered vulnerabilities, her confided marginality among the Jewish women who refused her pity or friendship, could not see into her feeling heart, did not understand how alone she was in this world protected as they were by husbands and respectability. The priest urged her to return and unburden herself once more. She went again, and yet again. Then the priest told himself he was making a house call to a parishioner in need.

"She bit him all up," my mother said. "He came for months. Then she got so wild she bit him all up. They saw the marks. They said to him, Where have you been? What could he say? They locked him up, there in the monastery."

"It's not a monastery, Ma." I said. "It's just a church near Gimbel's."

"Whatever the hell they call it," she said impatiently. She hated having the story line interrupted by a correction.

The priest did come for months, I remember that. He came late in the afternoon once, sometimes twice a week, but that spring evening when I saw them on the bed was probably the time she bit him all up, because I have no memory of the priest after that night.

It must have been iron in her mouth time after time. I remember the morning the chicken-store owner appeared at the door. Seven o'clock, and suddenly an immense noise out in the hallway. Mama pulled open the door and there

97

he was, Joseph Stalin standing in Nettie's doorway with a plucked chicken in one hand, Nettie in her nightgown with a second chicken in her hand, beating him about the face with the naked bird, shrieking, "For a chicken? You think I'll do it for a *chicken?*"

But everyone, Mama included, thought she was asking for whatever she got. She was considered provocative, suggestive, inviting. If you asked for specifics it was hard to get them. Foreheads would wrinkle, eyelids would narrow, mouths would purse. No one could say exactly what it *was* about her. On the other hand, no one backed down. It's not what she wears, one would say, it's the *way* she wears it. It's not what she says so much, it's the *way* she says it. It's not the expression on her face, it's sort of the whole face. You know what I mean? I can't put my finger on it, but I know what I mean. I would nod. I knew what they meant, too.

She had a way of walking up the block that had made me uncomfortable from the time I was ten years old. She walked like no other woman in the neighborhood. A woman's walk might be brisk or lazy, but inevitably it was the errand-bound walk of a housewife; her legs were attached to her torso for the strict purpose of useful locomotion, she was not walking to feel her body in motion or to have its movement acknowledged or responded to. Nettie was. Her walk was slow and deliberate. She moved first one haunch, then the other, making her hips sway. Everyone knew this woman was going nowhere, that she was walking to walk, walking to feel the effect she had on the street. Her walk insisted on the flesh beneath the clothes. It said, "This body has the power to make you want." There was nothing like her for a thousand miles around. Men and women alike hungered for her. It was awful. I could see she aroused strong emotion, but that emotion seemed bound up with punishment not privilege. The way people looked at her—the cruelty in the men, the anger in the women—made me fearful. I felt her in danger. Nettie walking up the block became woven into the fabric of early anxiety.

She, of course, was fearless. She took on all comers. Every pair of eyes on her was met by her own: wide, innocent, taunting. Sexual malice ran so deep in her it was an essence: primitive, calculating, stubborn; enraged at the center; made reckless by some burning imperative that pushed against a shifting outer limit, wholly determined by how bad she felt about herself and her life on any given day of the week. She knew of no other way to make herself feel better than to make people want her. She knew that when she swayed her hips, raised her eyelids slowly, brushed her hand languorously through her red hair, promise stirred in the groin. She *knew* this. It was all she knew. She thought this knowledge gave her power. She thought her own heartlessness *was* power. "You will feel and I will not feel," her swaying body said, "and that will make you weak and me strong." But she understood her situation only very imperfectly. She was, after all, a peasant from a village in the Ukraine with a limited grasp on things. Richie understood better than she what was actually going on, and one hot summer evening when I was seventeen and he was eight he showed me what he knew.

It was late August. Deep, serious heat. Cumulative heat that never entirely evaporated from the streets or from the apartments. You suffered the heat either intensely or less intensely. In the evening the worst of the midday swelter eased off and a weak breeze came through the windows propped open by wooden-framed screens. A convalescent sensuousness overtook the semidarkened rooms. We began to recover from the assault of the day.

I was sitting on the couch in the living room in a mood of dreamy exhaustion, trying to read in the last hour of daylight. Richie was sitting beside me, demanding attention. He was a beautiful child, dark-eyed, dark-haired, with high pink-and-white coloring, an irresistible smile, a voice like his mother's, soft and insinuating. He knew that in our house he had rights rather than obligations. This knowledge allowed him to move to the edge of brashness, although rarely did he cross a border from which he could not beat a safe retreat. On this particular evening, though, Richie *wanted* me to be with him. I elbowed him away, my eye not leaving the page. He refused my refusal.

"Richie," I said in exasperation, my eye still on the book. "Not now."

"Yes," he said. "Now."

"No!"

"Yes!"

I laughed, but kept on reading. Richie climbed onto my lap and began to play with the front of my dress, a brief halter-style affair, white and summer-thin, held closed by a zipper that stretched from neck to navel. I pushed weakly, inattentively, at his hands, still reading. He twined his arms around my neck and pressed his open lips against my throat. Startled, I felt his live mouth on me. I pushed seriously at him, but too late: he had sensed my hesitation. He held on to me, pressing himself against my chest as though now he had a right to me. He was strong, stronger than me. We began to fight as though we were both adults, or both children. Suddenly, in one incredible motion, Richie pulled the zipper of the dress all the way down, pushed one hand under my bra, the other under my panties. Before I realized what was happening, he had grasped my nipple between two fingers and was moving the middle finger of his other hand toward my groin. I went up like a tinderbox: instant convulsion of the body. In half a second I had his hands off me and was holding him out by the wrists, immobilized. I looked into his face, amazed. He looked back into mine. I could see in his face what he saw in mine. I could also see what he made of what he saw. His face was intent with triumph, interest, excitement. And behind the excitement something even more curious: a kind of sadness, a gravity. I thought of Richie five years old, strapped in a chair, staring at Nettie and the priest on the paisley-covered bed. He'd been growing wise since that night. He knew then his mother's life was not an exercise in power but an exchange of humiliations. Now he was just trying out what he knew.

A glorious day, today: New York hard-edged in the clear autumn sun, buildings sharply outlined against the open sky, streets crowded with pyramids of fruits and vegetables, flowers in papier-mâché vases cutting circles on the sidewalk, newspaper stands vivid in black and white. On Lexington Avenue, in particular, an outpouring of lovely human bustle at noon, a density of urban appetites and absorptions.

I have agreed to walk with my mother late in the day but I've come uptown early to wander by myself, feel the sun, take in the streets, be in the world without the interceding interpretations of a companion as voluble as she. At Seventy-third Street I turn off Lexington and head for the Whitney, wanting a last look at a visiting collection. As I approach the museum some German Expressionist drawings in a gallery window catch my eye. I walk through the door, turn to the wall nearest me, and come face to face with two large Nolde watercolors, the famous flowers. I've looked often at Nolde's flowers, but now it's as though I am seeing them for the first time: that hot lush diffusion of his outlined, I suddenly realize, in intent. I see the burning quality of Nolde's intention, the serious patience with which the flowers absorb him, the clear, stubborn concentration of the artist on his subject. I *see* it. And I think, It's the concentration that gives the work its power. The space inside me enlarges. That rectangle of light and air inside, where thought clarifies and language grows and response is made intelligent, that famous space surrounded by loneliness, anxiety, self-pity, it opens wide as I look at Nolde's flowers.

In the museum lobby I stop at the permanent exhibit of Alexander Calder's circus. As usual, a crowd is gathered, laughing and gaping at the wonderfulness of Calder's sighing, weeping, triumphing bits of cloth and wire. Beside me stand two women. I look at their faces and I dismiss them: middle-aged Midwestern blondes, blue-eyed moony. Then one of them says, "It's like second c[l]hood," and the other one replies tartly, "Better than anyone's first." I'm startled, pleasured, embarrassed. I think, What a damn fool you are to cut yourself off with your stupid amazement that *she* could have said *that*. Again, I feel the space inside widen unexpectedly.

That space. It begins in the middle of my forehead and ends in the middle of my groin. It is, variously, as wide as my body, as narrow as a slit in a fortress wall. On days when thought flows freely or better yet clarifies with effort, it expands gloriously. On days when anxiety and self-pity crowd in, it shrinks, how fast it shrinks! When the space is wide and I occupy it fully, I taste the air, feel the light. I breathe evenly and slowly. I am peaceful and excited, beyond influence or threat. Nothing can touch me. I'm safe. I'm free. I'm thinking. When I lose the battle to think, the boundaries narrow, the air is polluted, the light clouds over. All is vapor and fog, and I have trouble breathing.

Today is promising, tremendously promising. Wherever I go, whatever I see, whatever my eye or ear touches, the space radiates expansion. I want to think. No, I mean today I *really* want to think. The desire announced itself with the word "concentration."

I go to meet my mother. I'm flying. Flying! I want to give her some of this shiningness bursting in me, siphon into her my immense happiness at being alive. Just because she is my oldest intimate and at this moment I love everybody, even her.

"Oh, Ma! What a day I've had," I say.

"Tell me," she says. "Do you have the rent this month?"

103

"Ma, listen . . ." I say.

"That review you wrote for the *Times*," she says. "It's for sure they'll pay you?"

"Ma, stop it. Let me tell you what I've been feeling," I say.

"Why aren't you wearing something warmer?" she cries. "It's nearly winter."

The space inside begins to shimmer. The walls collapse inward. I feel breathless. Swallow slowly, I say to myself, slowly. To my mother I say, "You *do* know how to say the right thing at the right time. It's remarkable, this gift of yours. It quite takes my breath away."

But she doesn't get it. She doesn't know I'm being ironic. Nor does she know she's wiping me out. She doesn't know I take her anxiety personally, feel annihilated by her depression. How can she know this? She doesn't even know I'm there. Were I to tell her that it's death to me, her not knowing I'm there, she would stare at me out of her eyes crowding up with puzzled desolation, this young girl of seventy-seven, and she would cry angrily, "You don't understand! You have never understood!"

Mama and Nettie quarreled, and I entered City College. In feeling memory these events carry equal weight. Both inaugurated open conflict, both drove a wedge between me and the unknowing self, both were experienced as subversive and warlike in character. Certainly the conflict be-

104

tween Nettie and my mother seemed a strategic plan
surround and conquer. Incoherent as the war was, shot
through with rage and deceit, its aims apparently confused
and always denied, it never lost sight of the enemy: the
intelligent heart of the girl who if not bonded to one would
be lost to both. City College, as well, seemed no less con-
cerned with laying siege, to the ignorant mind if not the
intelligent heart. Benign in intent, only a passport to the
promised land, City of course was the real invader. It did
more violence to the emotions than either Mama or Nettie
could have dreamed possible, divided me from them both,
provoked and nourished an unshared life inside the head
that became a piece of treason. I lived among my people,
but I was no longer one of them.

I think this was true for most of us at City College. We
still used the subways, still walked the familiar streets between classes, still returned to the neighborhood each night,
talked to our high-school friends, and went to sleep in our
own beds. But secretly we had begun to live in a world
inside our heads where we read talked thought in a way
that separated us from our parents, the life of the house
and that of the street. We had been initiated, had learned
the difference between hidden and expressed thought. This
made us subversives in our own homes.

As thousands before me have said, "For us it was City
College or nothing." I enjoyed the solidarity those words
invoked but rejected the implied deprivation. At City College I sat talking in a basement cafeteria until ten or eleven
at night with a half dozen others who also never wanted
to go home to Brooklyn or the Bronx, and here in the
cafeteria my education took root. Here I learned that

105

Faulkner was America, Dickens was politics, Marx was sex, Jane Austen the idea of culture, that I came from a ghetto and D. H. Lawrence was a visionary. Here my love of literature named itself, and amazement over the life of the mind blossomed. I discovered that people were transformed by ideas, and that intellectual conversation was immensely erotic.

We never stopped talking. Perhaps because we did very little else (restricted by sexual fear and working-class economics, we didn't go to the theater and we didn't make love), but certainly we talked so much because most of us had been reading in bottled-up silence from the age of six on and City College was our great release. It was not from the faculty that City drew its reputation for intellectual goodness, it was from its students, it was from us. Not that we were intellectually distinguished, we weren't; but our hungry energy vitalized the place. The idea of intellectual life burned in us. While we pursued ideas we felt known, to ourselves and to one another. The world made sense, there was ground beneath our feet, a place in the universe to stand. City College made conscious in me inner cohesion as a first value.

I think my mother was very quickly of two minds about me and City, although she had wanted me to go to school, no question about that, had been energized by the determination that I do so (instructed me in the middle of her first year of widowhood to enter the academic not the commercial course of high-school study), and was even embattled when it became something of an issue in the family.

"Where is it written that a working-class widow's daughter should to go college?" one of my uncles said to her, drinking coffee at our kitchen table on a Saturday morning in my senior year in high school.

"Here it is written," she had replied, tapping the table hard with her middle finger. "Right here it is written. The girl goes to college."

"Why?" he had pursued.

"Because I say so."

"But why? What do you think will come of it?"

"I don't know. I only know she's clever, she deserves an education, and she's going to get one. This is America. The girls are not cows in the field only waiting for a bull to mate with." I stared at her. Where had *that* come from? My father had been dead only five years, she was in full widowhood swing.

The moment was filled with conflict and bravado. She felt the words she spoke but she did not mean them. She didn't even know what she meant by an education. When she discovered at my graduation that I wasn't a teacher she acted as though she'd been swindled. In her mind a girl child went in one door marked college and came out another marked teacher.

"You mean you're not a teacher?" she said to me, eyes widening as her two strong hands held my diploma down on the kitchen table.

"No," I said.

"What have you been doing there all these years?" she asked quietly.

"Reading novels," I replied.

She marveled silently at my chutzpah.

But it wasn't really a matter of what I could or could

not do with the degree. We were people who knew how to stay alive, she never doubted I would find a way. No, what drove her, and divided us, was me thinking. She hadn't understood that going to school meant I would start thinking: coherently and out loud. She was taken by violent surprise. My sentences got longer within a month of those first classes. Longer, more complicated, formed by words whose meaning she did not always know. I had never before spoken a word she didn't know. Or made a sentence whose logic she couldn't follow. Or attempted an opinion that grew out of an abstraction. It made her crazy. Her face began to take on a look of animal cunning when I started a sentence that could not possibly be concluded before three clauses had hit the air. Cunning sparked anger, anger flamed into rage. "What are you talking about?" she would shout at me. "What *are* you talking about? Speak English, please! We all understand English in this house. Speak it!"

Her response stunned me. I didn't get it. Wasn't she pleased that I could say something she didn't understand? Wasn't that what it was all about? I was the advance guard. I was going to take her into the new world. All she had to do was adore what I was becoming, and here she was refusing. I'd speak my new sentences, and she would turn on me as though I'd performed a vile act right there at the kitchen table.

She, of course, was as confused as I. She didn't know why she was angry, and if she'd been told she was angry she would have denied it, would have found a way to persuade both herself and any interested listener that she was proud I was in school, only why did I have to be such a showoff? Was that what going to college was all about? Now, take Mr. Lewis, the insurance agent, an educated man if ever there was one, got a degree from City College in 1929, 1929 mind you, and never made you feel stupid, always spoke in simple sentences, but later you thought about what he had said. That's the way an educated person should talk. Here's this snotnose kid coming into the kitchen with all these big words, sentences you can't make head or tail of . . .

I was seventeen, she was fifty. I had not yet come into my own as a qualifying belligerent but I was a respectable contender and she, naturally, was at the top of her game. The lines were drawn, and we did not fail one another. Each of us rose repeatedly to the bait the other one tossed out. Our storms shook the apartment: paint blistered on the wall, linoleum cracked on the floor, glass shivered in the window frame. We barely kept our hands off one another, and more than once we approached disaster.

One Saturday afternoon she was lying on the couch. I was reading in a nearby chair. Idly she asked, "What are you reading?" Idly I replied, "A comparative history of the idea of love over the last three hundred years." She looked at me for a moment. "That's ridiculous," she said slowly. "Love is love. It's the same everywhere, all the time. What's to compare?" "That's absolutely not true," I shot back. "You don't know what you're talking about. It's only an idea, Ma. That's all love is. Just an idea. You think it's a function of the mysterious immutable being, but it's not! There is, in fact, no such thing as the mysterious immutable being . . ." Her legs were off the couch so fast I didn't see them go down. She made fists of her hands, closed her eyes tight, and howled, "I'll kill you-u-u! Snake in my bosom, I'll kill you. How dare you talk to me that way?" And then she was coming at me. She was small and chunky. So was I. But I had thirty years on her. I was out of the chair faster than her arm could make contact, and running, running through the apartment, racing for the bathroom, the only room with a lock on it. The top half of the bathroom door was a panel of frosted glass. She arrived just as I turned the lock, and couldn't put the brakes on. She drove her fist through the glass, reaching for me. Blood, screams, shattered glass on both sides of the door. I thought that afternoon, One of us is going to die of this attachment.

Compounding our struggle, stimulating our anguish, swelling our confusion was sex. Me and boys, me and maidenhood, me and getting on with it. Safeguarding my virginity was a major preoccupation. Every boy I brought into the house made my mother anxious. She could not but leap ahead in her thoughts to the inevitable moment when he must threaten her vital interest. But she knew the danger came not so much from them as from me. With all her extraordinary focus on romantic love, and her sure knowledge that my generation of girls was made as miserable as her own over the loss of virginity before marriage, she nonetheless knew that something was loosed in me that had never been loosed in her; that she and I were not allies here in a common cause. If I came in at midnight, flushed, disheveled, happy, she'd be waiting just inside the door (she was out of bed as soon as she heard the key in the lock). She'd grasp my upper arm between her thumb and middle finger and demand, "What did he do? Where did he do it?" as though interrogating a collaborator.

Once, when she was positive I'd slept with the boy I'd gone out with, she pinched my arm until my eyes crossed in pain. "You've tasted him, haven't you," she said, her voice flat with accusation and defeat. That was her favorite euphemism for intercourse: "You've tasted him, haven't you." The phrase never failed to shock. I felt it in my nerve endings. The melodrama of repression, the malice of passivity, the rage over an absence of power, all of it packed into those words and I knew it from the first time I heard them. When she spoke them we faced each other across a no-man's-land of undefined but unmistakable dimension.

Nettie listened to us in amazement, and with transparent glee, convinced that every serious quarrel brought me closer to her. That year it became clear she had entered into competition with Mama for my allegiance. She wished to exert the primary influence over me. What she knew about men and women, life and the marketplace, education and the right husband would get me from the working-class part of the Bronx to the middle-class part of the Bronx. Every mother on the block knew that was the goal— Selma Berkowitz had the first nose job anyone had ever heard of because the Berkowitzes were planning to move to the Concourse and get her "a doctor for a husband"— and Nettie thought she could do better by me than any of these women. My mother? She was Anna Karenina. What did she know of maneuvering real life into position so that a girl could make the best bid? Nothing, absolutely nothing.

Nettie pushed my hair away from my face, stood back, and looked at me critically. "Your eyes are your best feature," she said. "Wear your hair so that everyone sees them right away." She straightened the skirt on my hips, the blouse on my shoulders. "Your figure is sexy," she said. "Wear simple clothes. No ruffles." Her eyes narrowed thoughtfully, and again came a piece of instruction on how to carry myself to best effect. She was arranging an object in a framed space. That, she said, was how a woman operated in the world. She arranged and presented herself, and what she hoped to get out of life was determined by the arrangement. Nettie wanted me to memorize her own arrangement only so that I might improve on it. She expected me to mimic and surpass her.

She knew that teaching me to be a seducer of men carried its own particular danger with it, but danger was not her province. Her province was preparing me for the best shot at life we could manage between us. It went without saying that if I became the hottest number on the block I'd be running the risk of rape and pregnancy, but those were the rules of the game, weren't they? A girl had to be *sensible*. Knowing how to give as little as possible to get as much as possible was something I should have taken in with mother's milk. My virginity was of no concern. Sooner or later I'd sleep with someone, no matter what she or anyone else said. The thing, of course, was pregnancy. That *would* be large trouble. Surely I didn't need instruc-

112

tion in how to avoid that, did I? I was a smart girl, a college girl. Now, let's see, green really *is* your color.

But none of it took. I was entranced during these woman-making sessions of ours. It was exciting, the way Nettie talked about men (her contempt was so educated!), and I loved watching her put herself together, but I couldn't concentrate on the task at hand, and its ultimate purpose remained an abstraction. I wanted to wear clothes the way she wore them, but I didn't want it enough. While I was with her I was absorbed by the glamour of costume-making, but away from her I'd lapse into my old forgetful habits of dress, couldn't remember what went with what, how to pull it all together. Certainly I couldn't remember that the way I dressed and held myself was a tool of the trade, an instrument of future gain, a vital means of achieving the image that would bring into my sphere of influence the man who could deliver up as much life-and-world as I had a right to hope for.

It wasn't that I doubted the necessity for such allure: who was I to doubt what all around subscribed to? Wasn't my mother as good as saying with every breath she drew, "Life without a man is unlivable"? And wasn't Nettie actually saying, "Men are scum but you gotta have one"? The message was not open to interpretation, a three-year-old could have repeated it: "If you don't get a husband you're stupid. If you get one and you lose him you're inept." I knew, beyond knowing, this was non-negotiable truth. Yet I couldn't pay attention. I was like the modern girl in the nineteenth-century novel: Yes, yes, but not right now.

113

Right now, only two things held my interest: talking books and ideas at school, and getting hot necking with Paul or Ralph or Marty in the hallway, on park benches, in the back seat of a car. A creature of immediate experience, I could not be compelled by the promised benefits of an unseen, unfelt future. But then again, who among us was so compelled? We were all creatures of immediate experience, none of us delayed gratification. Nettie *said* she was urging me to arrange myself so that I might secure a better piece of the action, but in fact she herself was hooked on the daily practice of allure. My mother *said* I needed love to experience life at a high level, but in fact mourning lost love was the highest level of life she had attained. We were all indulging ourselves. Nettie wanted to seduce, Mama wanted to suffer, I wanted to read. None of us knew how to discipline herself to the successful pursuit of an ideal, normal woman's life. And indeed, none of us ever achieved it.

Yet the idea of such a life never loosened its hold, and day by day, month by year, it drove each of us deeper into conflict. It was a given that the more uncertain we were, the more self-righteous we would become. It was necessary for each of us to feel special, different, destined for a superior end. Divided against ourselves, we withheld sympathy from one another. Secretly, each of us identified a collection of undesirable character traits in the others from which she separated herself, as though dissociation equaled deliverance. "Thank God, I'm nothing like *that*," each one said to herself of the others, at least once a day. But judgment did not bring amelioration. We could purge ourselves of neither fantasy nor rage. Beneath an intact surface each of us smoldered in silence. It was the smoldering that did us in. The quarrel between Nettie and Mama, when it broke out, moved with the speed of brushfire. Released from subterranean heat, it burned so hot, so fast, within seconds it had achieved scorched earth: on this ground nothing would grow again.

It's hard for me to remember when I first realized the tone of each woman had begun to alter severely when she spoke of the other, but one day my mother said, "All she does is switch her ass up and down the block. Why doesn't she go to work? It's a shame for all women, the way she carries on," and I looked up from the kitchen table (I was doing homework, she was at the ironing board). She had spoken such words often but, always before, the harshness had been cut by an exasperation in her voice that betrayed affection. Now the tone, like the words, was only hard.

"So she doesn't work," I said calmly. "So what? You object to her being on the dole?"

"It's not the relief I object to. It's the way she is with men. I think it's disgusting."

"You do? Most women envy the way she is with men. They wish they were as good at it as she is."

"I'd rather die than be that way with a man!" my mother said, the words bursting from her.

"No kidding," I murmured. "Die?"

She looked up from the ironing board, turned full face to me, and in a voice trembling with contempt said, "You're a child, you know nothing of life, nothing."

Suddenly I felt uneasy. What were we talking about? I mean, what were we *really* talking about? She had always felt constrained to temper her judgment of Nettie. Now

115

some recklessness was driving her to leave restraint behind. Why? What was making her so angry? The afternoon light, always mild in the kitchen, seemed to weaken perceptibly, grow pale and thin. Some tender threat rode the air. I shivered, and felt anxious. Melancholy pressed down on me.

One day during this same period of time Nettie and I were trying on some old dresses she had pulled out of the back of her closet. She put one on me, a clinging jersey, and at once we both saw how womanly my body had become. Nettie's hands came together in rapture. "Oh!" she gasped, "you look marvelous." Then she giggled like a mischievous child. "You wear that on the street, your mother will have a heart attack." I laughed, too, but beneath the laughter something clicked. That's right, I thought, she'd hate to see me in this dress, she'd consider it a betrayal.

"She'll say you look like a tramp," Nettie said. "She'll say you look like me." My head jerked toward her.

"She never said you look like a tramp."

"Maybe not, but she thinks it."

"Why do you say that?"

"Oh, come *on.*"

"You're wrong," I said. "She loves you. She worries about you."

"The way she worries about you when she pinches you till you see stars? 'What did he do, where did he do it?' "

I blushed and felt disloyal.

"She's jealous," Nettie said hotly. "Laying there on the couch all dried up, five years without a man's hand on her. You know what they say, don't you? You don't use

116

it, you lose it. That's your mother. She wants me to lose it, too. And you, also."

It wasn't the words that startled me. I'd heard them, or ones like them before. It was the bitterness in Nettie's voice: unexpected and unleavened. Again anxiety floated into the room, and again I felt threatened. Something sad and hopeless stirred in the air. It etherized me, this sad thing. I felt the energy evaporating in my body.

On a Sunday afternoon in late fall the three of us were in the kitchen. Nettie was fixing my hair in a new style and Mama, in a rare cooking mood, was making potato pancakes. The atmosphere was easy among us. Sarah had stopped by for an hour and, as always, had had some wonderful bit of gossip to bring in from the street. Today she had walked through the door saying, "Well, Mrs. Kerner is getting crazier by the minute. I just ran into her. You'll never believe what she said to me."

Mama supplied the rhetorical transition. "What did she say?"

"She said her pubic hair is on fire because the man downstairs is sending up radiation."

"Wha-a-at?" we all chorused.

Nettie laughed so hard I had to pull her back onto the bench.

"Migod, migod." Mama shook her head, a hand laid against a cheek. "They'll have to put her away soon."

"Did she actually say pubic hair?" I asked. Sarah nodded. "And radiation? She said radiation?" Again Sarah nodded. "See?" I was triumphant. "I *told* you she was a very intelligent woman."

Now, a couple of hours later, Mrs. Kerner was still on

our minds. Mama lifted the edge of a pancake out of the sizzling oil, peered at its underside, and announced, "That woman never should have stayed at home. She should have gone to work."

Beside me, Nettie stiffened. I, too, went on the alert. These words might be a prelude to the kind of veiled criticism Mama often made. Apparently talking about someone else, she would deliver a monologue, clearly aimed at Nettie, on the virtues of going to work.

"How could she have gone to work, Ma?" I asked. "She can't do anything."

"She could do, she could do. Everyone who wants to can do *something*."

"Something people will pay for? Mr. Kerner says he should get paid just for keeping her in the house." Without warning I had arrived at a piece of wisdom about marriage. "Come to think of it, that's exactly what he *does* get paid for. Why else does he work except to keep her in the house?"

Nettie laughed briefly. She was not yet sure of her position in this exchange.

"Very smart, very smart," my mother grumbled ominously. "If she would work he wouldn't have to keep her in the house. She wouldn't be crazy, and she could tell him to go to hell. Did you ever think about that, my brilliant daughter? That maybe she's crazy because she can't tell him to go to hell? When a woman can't tell a man to go to hell, I have noticed, she is often crazy."

Nettie was looking at her nails by now, smiling to herself. Mama turned unexpectedly away from the pancakes. She saw the smile.

118

"You think you tell them to go to hell, don't you," she said softly.

Nettie and I exchanged a quick glance. Mama saw the camaraderie, felt the exclusion.

"You think you're a hot shot because you won't go to work, don't you?" she shouted. "*Don't* you? Well, let me tell you something. You know what they say about you on the street?"

"Ma!"

Her face white, her lips compressed, a pulse beating in her neck, my mother struggled to gain control. Too late. Nettie herself had turned white and risen from the bench.

"What do they say about me on the street?" she asked, a dangerous smile in her voice.

"They say—"

"Ma! Stop it! Stop it!"

Nettie moved into the doorway of the kitchen. I moved with her. Mama moved toward both of us. Nettie stepped back into the foyer. So did I. Mama stepped between us. She laid conciliatory fingers on Nettie's arm. Nettie brushed the fingers from her arm and with one hand on the doorknob she hissed, "You know he always liked me."

For a moment that lasted a hundred years we remained as we were, the three of us, grouped in the tiny foyer. No one moved. My mouth opened and stayed open. Nettie's hand remained on the doorknob. Mama's fingers touched the air. The afternoon light, filled with threat and anxiety, fell on us from the distant kitchen window.

She slept with my father, I thought, and an immense excitement swept my body.

119

"You whore," my mother whispered. "You filthy whore. Get out of this house."

Nettie slammed out the door and Mama ran through the apartment. She flung herself down on the couch and wept hard, broken tears. Torn between pity and fascination, I watched her as long as she lay there. She cried for hours.

Months later I came home from school one evening at six o'clock. As I was about to insert my key in the lock, Nettie's door opened. "Come in," she pleaded. I stood with the key in my hand, staring at her. I could hear my mother moving about on the other side of our door. "Please," Nettie whispered again. "Just for a minute. She won't know." Her face was contorted with the effort that begging cost her. The key was half an inch from the lock. I don't remember what I thought, but I remember what I felt: If I go in to her I'm betraying Mama, if I don't I'm giving up sex. I went in.

I was so young. I had no way of knowing that to betray Mama was not to ensure that I would not give up sex.

"Why can't you find a nice man to be happy with?" my mother is saying. "Someone simple and good. Not an intellectual or a philosopher." We are walking down Ninth Avenue after a noon-hour concert at Lincoln Center. She

120

places one hand palm up in the air. "Why do you pick one shlemiel after another? Tell me. Do you do this to make me miserable? What *is* it?"

"For God's sake, Ma," I say weakly. "I don't 'pick' men. I'm out there, I'm just *out* there. Things happen, an attraction begins, you act on it. Sometimes, way in the back of your mind, for a fraction of a second, you think: Could this be serious? Is it possible this man will become my intimate? my partner? But mainly you push the thought away, because this is our *life*, Ma. Affairs. Episodes. Passions that run their course. Even when they include getting married."

She knows I'm speaking now from a losing position, and she moves right in.

"But an alcoholic?" she says.

"An ex-alcoholic, Ma."

"Alcoholic, ex-alcoholic, what's the difference?"

"Ma! He hasn't had a drink in four years."

"He also hasn't called in two weeks."

Marilyn Kerner had said almost the same thing. Marilyn (she never did get married), now forty-six, a lawyer living on the Upper West Side, remains a corrective voice in my life. When I want not the easy reassurance of the therapeutic culture but the unsparing appraisal of the standard-bearer of the Bronx, I call Marilyn. There are no euphemisms in Marilyn's vocabulary. Be prepared for an analysis that will strike like a body blow, or don't call Marilyn. But I had called Marilyn over this newest rapture of mine and she, too, had said, "An ex-alcoholic? Doesn't sound promising."

"But, Marilyn," I'd protested, "it's just the opposite. He's *been* there. He's been as powerless as a woman. He's got wisdom. Believe me. This man is extraordinarily unde-fended. The friendship between us has been marvelous. With every word, every gesture, every bit of behavior, he has said to me, 'I'm as vulnerable to this as you are, as sensitive to your fears and insecurities as I am to my own.' "

"But he hasn't been sensitive to his own," said Marilyn. "He's been pickled in alcohol for fifteen years."

"He's different now," I said. "Jesus Christ. Nobody gets a second chance in the Bronx, do they?"

"It's not that," Marilyn said. "It's that if you come from the Bronx you don't ignore the evidence. You can't afford to."

Now, of course, the evidence is weighing heavily against me. This man and I had met at a journalists' conference. Desire had flared quickly, and then happiness had taken us both by surprise. We had spent a month together. Now we had separated, I back to New York, he to the Midwest to finish an assignment. Our plan had been to meet in New York in six weeks. Meanwhile, he was to call the day after I got home. Two weeks have now passed: no phone call. He's on the road. I have no way of reaching him. It's been two weeks of concentrated misery. It's the first thing I'm aware of when I wake, the last thing before I sleep. I sleep so badly that often I'm awake in the night, where-upon I remember and the pain is dazzling. By now I'm not a character in a Doris Lessing story, I *am* a Doris Lessing story. The world is a framed space filled in by obsession. I move through the space grim and staring-eyed, a modern woman condemned to the knowledge that the experience of love will be played out repeatedly on an ever-diminishing scale, but always with a full complement of fever and sickness, intensity and denial.

Meanwhile, as we walk, the city is giving us back a street version of the drama raging within. We're in the Italian market district. All about us men are laboring to deliver cartonfuls of meat, vegetables, groceries. But in New York nothing gets separated out, so people's lives are also being delivered up on the street. A man standing at an open phone booth kicks insanely at the side of the booth while he shouts into the receiver, "I told you I'm coming! Didn't I *tell* you I'm coming? Why do you keep asking me if I'm coming?" At the corner three high-school girls, ferociously made up and dressed in polyester high fashion, are gathered in a tight knot. As we pass them one says to the other two, "I tell him, Tony, you leanin' too *hard* on me, I don' like no man to lean so *hard* on me."

My mother and I both listen carefully to the man on the phone and the girl on the corner. We walk two blocks without speaking. Then she peers sideways at me, and she says to me, "You know what the Russian says." No, I tell her, I can't say I do know what the Russian says. She speaks a sentence in Russian and translates, "If you want to go sleigh-riding you've got to be prepared to drag the sled." We both burst out laughing, and by the time I get home I'm feeling purged.

The phone is ringing as I walk into my apartment. It's Marilyn.

"Did he call?"

"No."

"Well . . ." she begins.

"I wrote him a letter," I say.

"A letter? What for?"

"To break the passivity, for one thing. It's awful, that helpless waiting. And also, I want him to know what I think of all this. I must say what I wrote is brilliant."

"Yes?" Marilyn says warily.

"Yes," I say. I choose not to hear the guardedness in her voice. "Want to hear some of it? I remember whole chunks."

"Sure."

"Well, I started out saying that although it was painful to me that his feelings hadn't lasted ten minutes in the real world I could absorb that, and live with it. What I couldn't absorb was his plunging us back into the cruelty of old-fashioned man-woman stuff, turning me into a woman who waits for a phone call that never comes and himself into the man who must avoid the woman who is waiting. I said I thought we'd been friends with a mutual interest in being civilized, reliable people even if we *were* in love."

"That's good," Marilyn says cautiously. "Very good."

"Now here's the brilliant part. I asked how it was possible that he hadn't been able to put himself in my place, imagine the pain and apprehension I'd be feeling, not be compelled to pick up the phone if only to say, 'Listen, I can't go on with this.' It was *this* I found offensive, even frightening. Now listen to this. I wrote: 'That failure of the sympathetic imagination, when it occurs between two people who have been intimate, is like natural disaster to me. It fills me with dread and amazement. The world then seems a barbaric place, without any hope of tender regard.' Isn't that great?"

124

Silence. Long, unexpected silence. Then Marilyn sighs. "You're still just like your mother," she says.

"What?" I yelp. "What do you mean?"

"You go on picking up these marginal types, idealizing them, and then you can't believe it when they don't know their place. You're amazed that they're doing this to *you*. Don't they know you're supposed to leave them, not they leave you? And then you get on your high horse."

"So how is that like my mother?"

"Your mother idealized a whole marriage, and when *it* left *her* . . . You can fill in the blank yourself."

My brother graduated and left the house, and Nettie did not cross our threshold. We were alone in the apartment, Mama and I, as I had always known we would be. She lay on the couch and stared into space. I hung out the window. Her stare was dull, silent, accusing. She would not be roused. I sat in the room, spoke the thoughts in my head, and nothing happened, absolutely nothing. It was as though I had not spoken. Her refusal was powerful. It hypnotized me, awed me into collaborative submission.

Failing to get what she wanted from life, what she thought she needed, felt was her due, my mother disappeared under a cloud of unhappiness. Beneath this cloud she felt helpless, fragile, and deserving of sympathy. When she was told her relentless melancholy was oppressive to those forced to witness it, she was surprised. Her mouth and eyes flashed angry hurt and she said, "I can't help it. This is how I *feel*. I can only act as I feel." Secretly she considered her depressed state a mark of sensitivity, of stronger feeling, finer spirit. She would not take in the idea that her behavior affected others adversely, and the notion that a certain level of social exchange is required below which no one has the right to fall was foreign to her. She could not see that her insistent unhappiness was an accusation and a judgment. "You?" it said with each resentful sigh. "You're not the right one. You cannot deliver up comfort, pleasure, amelioration. But you are my dearest of dears. Your appointed task is to understand, your destiny to live with the daily knowledge that you are insufficient to cure my life of its deprivation."

Before such superiority of will I lost myself entirely. The trick, of course, was that she couldn't be had. She wanted nothing; I wanted everything, anything. I raged and I railed at her ("The sun is shining! It's a sin to be indoors"), but inside I went numb and dumb, became languorous and stupid.

Affixed to our windows were old-fashioned guards made of strips of tin with curled edges at the tops that projected roundly into the air above the street, ballooning out in a kind of mock-balcony effect. The guards had been there when we came and would be there when we left, but I had not a sufficient sense of history to see the matter in this light and puzzled over why they were not taken down now that my brother and I were no longer children, never pausing to notice that I still made excellent use of them.

On weekend days I hung out the living-room window for hours on end, leaning deep into the inner curve of the guard, my back to the room, my mother lying on the couch behind me. It was much the same as when I sat on the window ledge at the other end of the room late at night with my legs on the fire escape, only one vital difference obtaining between the two window sittings. At night on the fire escape I fantasized grandly out into the world. During the day, leaning into the guard, I became the princess in the tower, a prisoner yearning down at the street below, my sense of remove then overpowering. I stared at people I knew (children playing, friends laughing, couples walking), as though across an immeasurable distance at a form of life foreign to me and permanently unavailable. To be one half of an ordinary human exchange taking place in the unbounded open seemed, during the hours I hung out the window, unthinkable. That is, unimaginable.

The imaginable had always been problematic. When I was a child the feel of things went into me: deep, narrow, intense. The grittiness of the street, the chalk-white air of the drugstore, the grain of the wooden floor in the storefront library, the blocks of cheese in the grocery-store refrigerator. I took it all so seriously, so literally. I was without imagination. I paid a kind of idiot attention to the look and feel of things, leveling an intent inner stare at the prototypic face of the world. These streets were all streets, these buildings all buildings, these women and men all women and men. I could imagine no other than that which stood before me.

That child's literalness of the emotions continued to exert influence, as though a shock had been administered to the nervous system and the flow of imagination had stopped.

I could feel strongly, but I could not imagine. The granite gray of the street, the American-cheese yellow of the grocery store, the melancholy brownish tint of the buildings were all still in place, only now it was the woman on the couch, the girl hanging out the window, the confinement that sealed us off, on which I looked with that same inner intentness that had always crowded out possibility as well as uncertainty. It would be years before I learned that extraordinary focus, that excluding insistence, is also called depression.

I stared out the window as though at a magical tableau, the granulated vacancy in the air behind me hanging like dead weight, pulling us both down to the bottom of all the years that had ever been or could ever be. We became, my mother and I, all women conditioned by loss, unnerved by lassitude, bound together in pity and anger. After Hiroshima dead bodies were found of people who had been wearing printed kimonos when they were killed. The bomb had melted the cloth on their bodies, but the design on the kimonos remained imprinted in the flesh. It seemed to me in later years the deep nerveless passivity of that time together had become the design burned into my skin while the cloth of my own experience melted away.

I began leaving home at nineteen and kept leaving until I was married in the living room at twenty-four in a noisy act of faith that announced the matter accomplished. My husband was small (my size); blond ("insignificant-looking," as Mama put it); foreign (he couldn't defend himself in English). We were drawn to each other by a common love

128

of the arts, but he was a visionary painter and in me literature had aroused the critical faculty. He was wordless, I was all words. In him repression was demonic, in me explosive. Most of the time he brooded, twice a year he drank himself into a stupor. I remained sober and a scornful tongue was my constant companion. All the differences were negotiable except one: I talked better than he did and I used words like a weapon. That knocked us hopelessly off balance. I opened my mouth and power was mine: I could slice, cut, and pin; thrust, batter, and storm. He was helpless before the amazing siege. To the very largest degree that must have been how I wanted it, although certainly I could not then see this simple reality driving me on in all my attachments to men. The course I had followed to lead me to this man and this marriage was not difficult to trace (any child analysand could have delivered a creditable description of the psychological terrain), but I remained deep in the woods a quarter of a mile from the road.

A woman in the movement once said, "We were all either stars or groupies." By groupies she meant the women who had swum in the orbit of the ordinarily accomplishing men they had married and stayed married to. By stars she meant the rest of us: those who bucked and kicked against the allotted destiny, could neither make a proper marriage nor walk away from marriage altogether. I remember entering graduate school at Berkeley and being confronted for the first time by the two kinds of women who conformed to this model. Later I realized it was all there, in that small tight world, relations between the sexes as I would ever know them.

The English department at Berkeley was itself a model for human relations in the world. There were those in power: the brilliant, famous, full professors, and those seeking power: the brilliant young men ready to become the disciple, the protégé, the son and intellectual companion. Together, professor and protégé formed the interlocking links in the chain of civilized cronyism that ensured the ongoingness of the enterprise being served: English literature in the university.

Side by side with the young men were the women students. Most of them came from the Midwest, wore Peter Pan collars, were choked silent with intensity, and in the third year at school became engaged to one of the promising young men. Many of these women were also brilliant: one wrote intellectual poetry, another psychoanalyzed Henry James, a third reinterpreted *The Faerie Queen*. It was interesting to observe how people in the department spoke of such a woman once she became one half of the future academic couple. Before she had not really been spoken of at all. Now she was referred to in muted tones, as though the conversants were in a sickroom speaking of an invalid, and inevitably one heard one of them saying, "Poor Joan. Gifted girl, really. Of course it's unthinkable that she not marry Mark, who is, after all, brilliant and will carry her into the only life worth having; but what she could have done." The mixture of ritual and relief in the speaker's voice was both peculiar and palpable.

Then there were the other women students. Intense in an altogether different way. Brash, difficult, "gypsy-dark" (meaning Jewish from New York), the intelligence strong not subtle, the sensibility aggressive not demure, the manner startling in its overdirectness, without grace or modesty, disorienting. These women did not fall in love with Mark, who sat next to them in Medieval Lit 101. They studied with him, argued with him, sometimes slept with him, but they did not marry him. Or he them. To Mark these women were exotics, a temporary stimulation to be indulged before one got down to real life. To the women Mark was an ambitious drone, clever but cautious, wanting adoration without an argument. In short, these hungry young people feared, despised, and excited one another. Secretly, I think, most of them yearned to make connection. But the secret remained a well-kept one.

The men were able to retreat from anxiety into a readymade identity. They got their Ph.D.'s, married Joan, and went off to walk the carefully prepared road that had been assigned them. The women had no such luck. Who were they to identify with? Where were they to go? At Berkeley I know where they went. They fell into affairs with married professors, black activists, antisocial mathematicians; or they hung out at the bars on the other side of Shattuck Avenue (Berkeley's social divider), where one met adventurers rather than graduate students: bartenders, painters, poetic drifters, fishermen down from Alaska, pot growers in from Oregon. Their lives were fractured. By day they were absorbed by Renaissance poetry and the life of the English department; by night they slept with men who crossed Shattuck Avenue on a twenty-four-hour visa. Sexual adventure was an event that only rarely converted into experience. In some important way these women remained as innocent of life, of their own lives, as did Mark and Joan whiling the years away in one remote university town or another.

I need hardly say among which group I took my own uneasy place. I had come to Berkeley also trailing a list of "inappropriate" attachments. I already knew I had hopeless trouble with the Marks of this world, trouble I thought originated in their insecurities, their fears, their defenses. Me, I was ready. It was they who didn't want a wife who talked back, they who were afraid of a woman like me. The contempt poured into those words "afraid of a woman like me." Such fear was low, cunning, perverse, scurvy and wormlike. A man who was afraid of a woman like me deserved the kind of tongue-lashing that would leave him paralyzed from the waist down.

I didn't hang out on the other side of Shattuck Avenue, but I managed often enough to find the men with that combination of weakness and strength required to release sexual attraction. Real satisfaction, of course, was never achieved. Something was always wrong with these liaisons. Mary McCarthy had written of the men her own fictional surrogate fell in love with: If they were clever they were funny-looking, if they were virile they were stupid. That equation read like hard-won wisdom to me, and to many of my friends. We quoted McCarthy at one another triumphantly. Her elegant phrasing elevated our condition from the level of complaint to that of fixed truth.

What I could not register was this: In each of these affairs a necessary element of control devolved on me. If a man was short or stupid or uneducated or foreign, I felt sufficiently superior to risk tenderness. I might be socially

132

uncomfortable but I was freed up. Love was a swamp of overwhelming proportion. It covered the ground once I stepped off the solid territory of miserable, blessed loneliness. To sleep with a man was to start drowning in need. An equalizer was an absolute, not a relative an absolute necessity.

Stefan was neither stupid nor uneducated, but he was short and foreign and an artist. He groped for words, his English was not fluent, he did work I could not evaluate but could nonetheless be skeptical of. He was also a lapsed Catholic endowed with a missionary zeal for painting that appealed strongly to my own burning moralism. This tipped the balance toward marriage. We met one night at a party in North Beach, not far from the art school where he was a student, and immediately began to discuss the significance of Art, the privilege of being allowed to serve, the promise and the glory, the meaning and the transcendence. The conversation mesmerized us. We met repeatedly to hear ourselves speak the magic words again and again. Very quickly I began to image a life together, intense and high-minded, devoted to the idea of the Great Work.

And he? What did he want from me? The same, the very same. I, apparently, fitted perfectly into the landscape of *his* imagined life. I was a graduate student in literature: that was good. I was a fierce moralizing Jewess: that was better. I worshipped at the shrine of Art: that was best. We told each other that with the stability of a life together we would each do the large work we knew we were meant to do. It was a marriage born of spiritual fantasizing. We did not want each other, chemically or romantically. The misery that had to be lived out before that simple knowledge was ours.

I called home and announced I was getting married. At the other end of the phone my mother was speechless. When she found her tongue it was to revile me for bringing her a goy. *But, Ma! We were communists!* She calmed down, asked me when I was coming back to New York and what kind of a wedding I wanted. Homemade, I laughed. *Thanks, Ma.*

I came back and she gripped me in a hard, angry embrace. She *did* try, but repeatedly her head filled with blood, over what, I think she hardly knew . . . oh yes, I was marrying a goy. I was elated. I began to feel embattled. Now I wanted to marry Stefan more, I thought, than I would ever again want anything. I must fight for the integrity of my opposed love, fight her to the death. But each day at noon I was overcome by a wave of nausea, and chaos beat inside *my* head. What was I doing? Why was I getting married? Why was I marrying *him*? Who was *he*? I was going to stand up before a judge and swear, call this man husband, take his name . . . I felt myself plunging . . . Don't think about it, it's too late now, all too late. If she wins this one you are lost.

An immense activity overtook our kitchen the day before the wedding. Everyone pitched in: Sarah, Mrs. Zimmerman, Marilyn and her mother, cleaning, cooking, laughing, talking. When I think back on it, the only spontaneous fun occurred the day before, in the kitchen, preparing for the festivity. That is, *they*, the other women,

134

had fun. Not me and Mama. Mama's face was a mask of tension. She worked hard and well, was helpful to everyone, answered when spoken to, but a cloud of depression surrounded her. The live, warm presence of my mother had disappeared. In its place stood this remoteness posing as Mama. Her anxiety was unbearable to me. It made me crazy. I needed her to respond, to be there with me. I *needed* it. Not getting what I needed, I fell into an anxiety of my own that rendered me nearly speechless. Sick with fear and panic, I wandered about the room smiling wanly: trying so *hard*, I thought. We became a pair of matched performers in the kitchen. The other women gave us a wide berth, speaking carefully to each of us, as one does to the potentially unbalanced. Enraged, I thought, This bitch is spoiling everything for everyone. But then I saw that the conversation of the others was as lightheartedly crude, as briskly outrageous as ever. Only I was being brought down. Only I was responding to Mama's mean misery with an even meaner one of my own.

In the late afternoon we suddenly ran out of flour and sugar. Mama pulled off her apron and said she needed air, she would go to the grocery store. I couldn't let her out of my sight. "I'll come with you," I said. She nodded wordlessly, as though she had expected no less.

We left the house and trudged up the block. It was late August. I was wearing a thin dress that was one summer too old. The hem had come down that very morning and I had pinned it up. Now as we walked a mild breeze rippled the dress, exposing the pins. My mother said sharply, "What *is* that?" I followed her gaze. "The hem came down

135

this morning." I shrugged. "I couldn't find the sewing box."
Right then and there, on the street, halfway between the
house and the grocery store, she lost her mind.

"You are dis*gus*ting!" she yelled at me. "Disgusting! Look
at you. Just look at you. You're a mess! That's what you
are. A mess! When will you ever learn? You think you'll
learn? You won't learn." People began to turn around.
She didn't notice. Suddenly her body trembled. Her skin
lost its color. She pushed her face at mine. "He'll never
marry you," she hissed.

The pain in my chest cracked open, and an angry
frightened excitement ran quickly into the cleared space.
She was jealous, great God, she was jealous. It wasn't just
that I was getting married, it was that the glamorous goy
was taking me out into the world. I could see it in her
eyes. We stood there, immobilized. I felt my face going
gray like hers. Without another word, we turned away from
each other and continued on to the grocery store.

From the cake to the music to the clothes, the wedding
was indeed homemade. We pushed the furniture into the
bedrooms, threw open the glass doors between the two
middle rooms, set up a table of food at one end, a friend
who played the accordion at the other, and in between a
mob of people ate, drank, and danced, whooping with ceremonial high spirits. Very quickly, the atmosphere gener-
ated warmth, intimacy, filial affection. The only strangers
at the wedding were Stefan and I. We stood together on
an island in the middle of the room. On this island each
of us was alone. He didn't have a friend in sight, and all
the Yiddish made him horribly uncomfortable. I did have

a friend in sight, but the strain in his face separated me from my friends. What had drawn us together and urged us into this moment had suddenly become a desperate abstraction. We could neither join nor counteract the power of the inherited ritual being acted out on our behalf. Completing my isolation was the sight of Mama in continual food-supplying motion, her eyes grim, on her mouth a fixed smile, her hand out palm up warding off congratulations.

Stefan and I returned to California and set about making a home out of a five-room flat in North Beach. The place was a shambles (crumbling walls, flaking ceilings, broken floors), but the rooms were shapely and the light transforming, and I think we thought at the end of that project we would be real married people. We set to work with hearts that were actually lightened by the prospect of the work ahead of us, hearts made heavy now each day and each night as we tried to negotiate the terrifying reality to which an errant impulse had joined us. For the first time we saw how foreign we were to one another. I had not a bohemian bone in my body, he had not an unrebellious one in his. I could not bear incoherence in the physical surround, he could not bear a room that seemed finished. I cherished clarity of thought, he was drawn to mystic revelation. Each day brought long moments of unhappiness it took hours to recover from. Each night we took to bed our confusion, our longing, our paralyzing intensity. Only rarely did our bodies give us relief, and then but for an hour. It was my first experience of sexual love as catharsis, wherein one is left as lonely in the morning as one had been the evening before.

The apartment was rich in overall space, but each room was comparatively small. The problem this presented was Stefan's studio. We had agreed when we married that, to consolidate our life and to save us money, he would give up the spacious basement studio he'd been living in and make his studio in the apartment. A towerlike room with windows all around at the farthest end of the flat had seemed ideal. Now suddenly we realized how little floor space the tower room actually contained. Oh well, we'd take the matter under consideration when we got to it. Meanwhile, we decided we would start in the kitchen right near the front door and steadily work our way through the place. That, I said, was the logical thing to do. Yes, Stefan agreed, that *was* the logical thing to do. When I think back on it: room by room we carved out the distance, measured the drift, implemented the loss.

It was a large old-fashioned working kitchen with three tall windows, a wide shallow basin set high in a wooden counter, and a built-in bench and table. We plastered and painted and laid linoleum. When the room was finished, and the table and bench gleaming white, Stefan painted a broad band of orange around the rim of the table. That orange. On the most painful of days that orange, hard and brilliant, lifted my heart, cleared my spirit. Often, when I remember the apartment, it's the orange band around the kitchen table I see first. Then the murk comes crowding in.

The kitchen was where I first began to grasp the mean-

138

ing of the word wife. Here we were, a pair of twenty-four-year-olds: one day we're a graduate student and a working artist, the next day we're a wife and a husband. Before, we had always put the rude meals we ate on the table together. Now, suddenly, Stefan was in his studio each evening drawing or reading, and I was in the kitchen struggling to prepare and serve a meal we both thought should be proper. I remember taking an hour and a half to prepare some godawful casserole dish out of a woman's magazine, the two of us wolfing it down in ten minutes, then me taking an hour to clean up the mess, staring into the sink thinking, Is this it for the next forty years?

I discovered that I loathed cooking: could not absorb its social value, puzzled endlessly over why it should fall to me to provide this service we both required equally, and remained willfully inept for a much longer time than was necessary. Yet, one morning three months after we'd been married, Stefan said to me, "You make the lousiest coffee," and I was stricken. Neither of us had ever cared before about good coffee, or about who had provided the coffee, good or otherwise. Now, suddenly, the bad coffee on the table was a deficiency of mine. Driven to correct this stated failure, I walked into an Italian café down the block and said mournfully to the retired men hanging out, "My husband says I make lousy coffee." They gathered around me immediately. One said it was the packaged coffee, one said it was the pot, one said it was the water. I bought a drip pot, unground coffee beans, bottled water. Still, the coffee was lousy. Too weak, too strong, too mild, too bitter: sometimes interesting never delicious. One night at a party a painter twice my age said tiredly to me, "It's all in the measurements. Just measure accurately and I guarantee it will come out fine." He was right. I learned to measure, and the coffee misery ended as suddenly as it had begun: as though I had driven through a patch of fog on a night when visibility is already low.

It was a measure of youth and ignorance that we swallowed whole these clichéd responses to the words husband and wife. Our own fantasies of normality did not tend in this direction. As we moved from bedroom to living room to study and studio, we felt more and more acutely the real difficulty of the course we had set ourselves on, the magic that getting married was meant to perform. We saw ourselves primarily as people ardent about creative work. The redone apartment was to be a declaration of intent; it was to mirror our high-minded solidarity. But somehow the place refused to come together. We couldn't figure out why. Each completed room seemed to hang in space, remain distinctly separate, without flow or intimacy. We puzzled—I know Stefan did as much as I—over what was going wrong, but we were in no position to do more than puzzle. We kept drifting up and down that central hallway, in and around those many-windowed rooms, in search of an elusive integration we must have felt we had mislaid somewhere.

Nearly all graduate-student apartments were filled with Mexican pottery, straw rugs, madras spreads. I suggested we avoid all that. The bedroom, for instance, I said, should be cool and refreshing, a place of retreat and recovery. (From what, I now wonder.) "Let's paint the walls light gray," I said, "trim the windows in white, and cover the bed with a blue-gray cotton spread." Stefan thought that original and promptly set to work with me to realize the scheme, but when we were done something didn't sit right. The room was not a pleasant place to enter. Again, we puzzled. Every single thing in it was indeed so pretty. That it was a room in which nightly we re-enacted our failure to connect, that the light-gray walls were sprayed with loneliness and the blue-gray cotton spread never wrinkled by spontaneity, those were thoughts for which we literally had no sentences.

It was the same with my study. We bought an old wooden table I thought would make a good desk, and a slatted chair to go with it. We built bookshelves, nailed up a bulletin board, put a rocking chair near the window, and again chose a color for the room I thought quiet but lively. Now, we both said, now I would work. But the table was too high and too thick, the chair felt clumsy and rigid, the bulletin board remained oddly naked, and the color made me anxious: a beige that had been warm in the can turned aloof on the wall. Then there was the matter of the books. Stefan had suggested we integrate our books, and to my own amazement I heard myself say, "No. I want to keep my books separate." He had flushed deeply, and gone silent. I saw that I had hurt him and my first impulse was to take back what I had said, but the impulse was not whole and I did not act on it. The books in the study remained mine alone, but I no longer took pleasure in looking at them. When I sat in the rocking chair, my eye scanning the shelves for something to read, I felt a dull pain remembering how hard Stefan had worked to put the shelves together and help me arrange the books. The pain made it difficult to read, or even to think, in this room.

141

The living room was a holding action. I think we both knew that even then. Here we put down a straw rug, stuck paper flowers in clay pots, tossed a brightly striped covering on the daybed-couch. The only original touch in the room was not functional. We found a glass coffee table in a Goodwill store. The glass was discolored, the wooden base badly nicked. Stefan sanded down the wood. He poured a thick stream of sienna paint onto the glass top, and another stream of white. Then he sat down beside the table with a brush in his hand and began to direct the two streams of paint in circular motions, like a conductor with an orchestra, laughing delightedly but working with concentration (any application of paint deserved serious attention). The result was a vibrant abstraction sitting horizontally in the middle of the room. The paint was so wonderfully encrusted no coffee cup had a sliding chance.

The painted table, like the orange band, was a spot of brightness that made vivid the unhappy gloom mounting up in those oddly shaped rooms with the light pouring in from fifteen windows. In principle we agreed on everything, but in the dailiness of life we never seemed to want the same thing at the same time. We each came to think of ourselves as always making do or giving in. Invariably, one of us felt pushed out of shape. All I want is a normal life! I cried to myself. Why is everything so hard? Why are we always angry or intense? in hurt disagreement over this, that, or the other?

My own behavior seemed perfectly reasonable to me. Stefan's was perplexing. Stubborn and dug-in, I thought. On Sundays especially. Sundays Stefan spent the entire day in his studio (first at the school, then later at home).

142

"But Sunday," I protested. "That's the day we're supposed to spend together." What else did I get married for? I was thinking. "This I cannot bargain with," he said. "I must spend the day in my studio. I stare at the canvas, I study the work, I am restored. I cannot go on with the week unless I have this day to myself. Try to understand." "How about part of the day?" I wheedled. "Work in the morning and walk with me in the afternoon." He looked at me, his blue eyes cold and unreadable. "No," he said. "I need the whole day." Then he said, "Why don't you work, too?" It was my turn to look blank. "But it's Sunday," I repeated. The coldness gave way to mockery. "Only a *bourgeois* must go walking on Sunday," he said, "not an artist." At that I'd slam out the door.

On the Friday morning when we were to begin work on Stefan's studio we quarreled openly, over what I no longer recall, but I was deeply stung by the exchange. Instead of going off with him to plaster and paint (as he had done with me in my study, and in every other room in the house), I retreated into a dark depression from which I could not rouse myself. For three days I was unable to respond, very nearly unable to speak. I wandered aimlessly about the apartment or walked the city streets. Stefan went to the studio by himself. Whenever I left the apartment or returned to it, I looked straight down the central hall into the open doorway where I could see him working hour after hour in lonely silence, high up on a ladder, scraping at the tops of the tall window frames in that round room suffused with light. I was flooded with regret. I longed to be extricated from my own tightness, cajoled into reconciliation. Only later did I realize how enraged Stefan must have been by my refusal to work on his room when he would never have refused, no matter how he felt, to work on mine. He did not speak. I did not speak.

On Monday I recovered the power of speech and began to work alongside him in the studio, but we did not clear out inside. We were polite to one another at dinner, and even for an hour afterward in the living room. Then he went to bed and I stayed up reading. When I lay down beside him, he was either asleep or pretending to be asleep. In the days that followed, the awful politeness gave way to a kind of strained considerateness. The strain, like low-grade infection, was bearable. We accustomed ourselves to an atmosphere of domestic tension I thought would dissipate momentarily. I'd wake up and say to myself: "Today. Today it comes to an end." But then I'd get out of bed and the air would start filling up with that mild molecular misery.

I sat in the rocking chair staring into space. Stefan came into the room and suggested we go for a walk. I lifted the book from my lap and said no, I had to finish the chapter. The next night he suggested a movie. No, I said, I was too tired. The third night there was a party at the school. "You go," I said, "I'm really not in the mood." He stood in the doorway and looked at me for a long moment. Then he began to shout.

"Whatever I offer, it's not right! Or maybe it's just that I'm not right. Eh? Is that it? No matter what I do it can't be right because I'm not the right one. Isn't that so? That's what you make me feel. All the time. Not just now. All the time. You're always dissatisfied, always disappointed. With everything. You don't work to make things better,

144

you just sit in that damned rocking chair looking disappointed."

My mother and I are walking past the Plaza Hotel at noon, on our way to eat lunch in the park. Gathered around the fountain in front of the hotel a swarm of people: sitting, standing, strolling out to the sidewalk to buy shish kebab, soda, pretzels, falafel, egg roll, and hot dogs. They are eating out of tinfoil, drinking out of plastic, being entertained by street performers who pass the hat: break dancers, mimes, string quartets. One of the street performers not passing the hat is a fundamentalist preacher pacing back and forth in front of the fountain, thundering at individual people: "You are going straight to hell! Not tomorrow, not tonight, *right now!*" He makes the mistake of stopping my mother. She dismisses him with a brusque "What's *your* problem?" (she can't spare the time for this one), and keeps walking.

I laugh. I'm exhilarated today. Today *I'm* a street performer. I've always admired the guts, the skill, the command of the one who plays successfully to the passing New York crowd. Last night I spoke at a large public meeting in the city: on the barricades for radical feminism, also not passing the hat. I spoke easily and well, and I had the crowd in my hand. Sometimes I don't, but last night I did. Last night all the skill I've acquired at this sort of thing was there at my command, and I knew it. It was the know-

145

ing it that made me clear-headed, lucid, expansive and expressive. The crowd was being stirred. I felt it, and then I had confirmed what I felt.

My mother was in the audience. I didn't see her afterward, because I was surrounded and carried off. Today, right now, is our first meeting since I walked onstage last night. She is smiling at me now, laughing with me at the pleasure of the day, the crowd, New York acting out all over the place. I am properly expectant. She is about to tell me how wonderful I was last night. She opens her mouth to speak.

"Guess who I dreamed about last night," she says to me. "Sophie Schwartzman!"

I am startled, taken off balance. This I had not expected. "Sophie Schwartzman?" I say. But beneath my surprise a kernel of dread begins growing in the bright bright day.

Sophie Schwartzman had lived in our building for some years, and she and Mama had been friends. After the Schwartzmans moved to another neighborhood in the Bronx our two families had continued to meet because the women liked each other. The Schwartzmans had three children: Seymour, Miriam, and Frances. Seymour became a famous composer who changed his name to Malcolm Wood. Miriam grew up to become her mother. Frances, a pretty girl with "ambitions," married a rich man. Sophie has been dead a good ten years now. I haven't seen any of her children in more than twenty years.

"I dreamed I was in Sophie's house," my mother says, crossing Fifty-ninth Street. "Frances came in. She had written a book. She asked me to read it. I did, and I wasn't

146

so enthusiastic. She became very angry. She screamed at her mother, 'Never let her come here again.' I felt so bad! I was sick at heart. I said, 'Sophie. What is this? You mean after all these years I can't come here anymore?' " My mother turns to me as we reach the sidewalk and, with a huge smile on her face, says, "But then it was so wonderful! I woke up, and it was only a dream."

My feet seem to have lead weights in them. I struggle to put one in front of the other. My mother doesn't notice that I have slowed up. She is absorbed by her own amazing narrative.

"You dreamed this last night, Ma?"

"Yes."

"After I spoke?"

"Well, yes, of course. Not *right* after. When I got home and went to sleep."

We enter the park, find a bench, sit down, take out our sandwiches. We do not speak. We have each fallen into reverie. After a while my mother says, "Imagine dreaming about Sophie Schwartzman after all these years."

One night when Stefan and I had been married a little more than a year the phone rang at midnight. I picked up the receiver, said hello, and at the other end Mama's voice sobbed my name.

"What's happened, Ma?" I cried. "What is it?"

"Nettie," my mother wept. "Nettie. She's dead!"

"Oh, Ma! Omigod."

"Cancer. She had a cancer in the stomach."

"I didn't even know she was sick."

"Neither did I. It all happened so fast. You know I don't talk to her, I haven't been next door in years, I didn't know anything. She had stomach pains for weeks. Finally they got so bad Richie rang my bell and asked me to call the hospital. So then I went in. She was laying there doubled up, howling like an animal. The ambulance came, they took her away. Three weeks she lasted. She died this afternoon."

"Did you see her in the hospital?"

"No. I didn't."

"Why not?"

"I couldn't go. I just couldn't."

"That lousy pride of yours."

"Ah-h-h," she said. I could see her hand cutting the air beside the telephone. "You're such a child. You understand nothing."

"I understand you let her die alone with no one beside her except Richie. That I understand very well."

Silence. At both ends.

"I couldn't go to her. I just couldn't."

More silence.

"She was rotten inside," Mama said. "Eaten up. All those men, they ate her up."

"For God's sake, Ma! Do you really believe that? You think sex gives you cancer?"

"She had a cancer, didn't she?"

"Oh, Ma."

"Don't 'oh, Ma' me. I know what I'm talking about."

148

I hung up and lay back carefully. A solid weight had settled on my chest. If I moved too quickly, or perhaps at all, I'd have the breath crushed out of me. Stefan was touched by what he had heard. He stroked my face and shoulders and kissed me many times. Then he stroked my breast, my belly, my thighs. Suddenly a violent eroticism was upon us. We made hard love, and I cried. The weight lifted.

For the moment I was released from the pain of Nettie's death, but not from the shadowy guilt she herself aroused in me. As I lay back for the third time that night, I saw Nettie's face floating in the dark before me, as always its lips pressed together, its eyes a flat stare of disapproval. Invariably, her recalled image made me feel anxious, and oddly shameful.

In the years between the time she and Mama had quarreled and the time I had married, I hardly thought of Nettie at all. I didn't have to. Like the apartment, the furniture, the street, she was simply there, even though we rarely saw one another (this quarrel was my first demonstration of the psychological distribution of shared space). After my marriage Nettie seemed continually to be at the edge of my thoughts, especially when Stefan and I made love. Then I felt the force of her presence most acutely and most disapprovingly. She would materialize in the air, as if to say, "For this I wasted my hard-won knowledge on you?"

For a long time, a few years in fact, Stefan and I described the tension between us as intensity. (Tension we knew was in the negative, but intensity—ah, intensity!) Our lovemaking was almost invariably tight and explosive, a pent-up release from the gloom that marked so many of our days. The atmosphere of our early quarrels had never actually dissipated; bit by bit we had accustomed ourselves to it, as one does to a weight on the heart that constricts freedom of movement but does not preclude mobility: soon enough walking about in the cramped position seems natural. An absence of lightheartedness between us became the daily condition. We could live with it, and unfortunately we did. Not only did we live with it, we fell into the habit of describing our difficulty as a matter of intensity.

The difficulty was chronic, not occasional. Every other day some little thing would set one of us off. There would be an inconsiderate exchange and we would each feel hurt. Instead of airing the hurt quickly and openly, neither of us spoke. Minutes hours days passed in silence. By the end of a week the anxiety was stifling. Each morning we separated in relief, I to the English department across the bay, Stefan to the art school up on the hill. During the day my sense of grievance invariably melted. Overcome with tender affection, I would plan to walk through the door, throw my arms about Stefan, cover his face with kisses, and say, "What *is* this nonsense?" But when I *did* walk through the door his face seemed made of stone, and the first thing I heard him say was "You left the cap off the toothpaste this morning"; whereupon I'd turn on my heel, walk into the kitchen, make a cup of coffee, and disappear into my study. Sometimes Stefan came into the kitchen while I was preparing the coffee. I would see a thick vein pulsing in his neck as he drank a glass of water, or two white spots standing on his cheeks. But I would not speak and neither would he. I'd leave the room with my coffee as though I had important work to do. Then I'd carefully leave the door of the study half open. If he passed by he'd see me sitting in the rocking chair, staring into space, a perfect picture of accusation and misery. At last, when the air was so thick we could hardly breathe, one of us would break through. More often than not it was Stefan. He would sink to his knees before the rocking chair, wrap his arms around my legs, and murmur, "What is it? Tell me." Then I'd burst into tears, cry, "I can't go on like this! I can't work! I can't think!" And we'd go to bed.

It was always "I can't work! I can't think!" That was the holy invocation between us, the litany, the chant, the ceremonial admission that eroticized and restored. Either he would rage, "I can't work!" or I would, and that phrase punctured the compression chamber into which we had sealed ourselves. The inability to work was the only unembarrassed, unafraid admission we could make to one another. In the act of announcing this frailty we reminded ourselves of the superior nature of our common sensitivity and felt safe from the judgment we each feared in the other. To be wretched in the name of work was ultimately to armor ourselves against each other.

Yet those years were a true beginning for me. I did actually try to sit at the desk and think. Mostly, I failed miserably. Mostly, not always. In the second year of my marriage the rectangular space made its first appearance inside me. I was writing an essay, a piece of graduate-student criticism that had flowered without warning into thought, radiant shapely thought. The sentences began pushing up in me, struggling to get out, each one moving swiftly to add itself to the one that preceded it. I realized

151

suddenly that an image had taken control of me: I saw its shape and its outline clearly. The sentences were trying to fill in the shape. The image was the wholeness of my thought. In that instant I felt myself open wide. My insides cleared out into a rectangle, all clean air and uncluttered space, that began in my forehead and ended in my groin. In the middle of the rectangle only my image, waiting patiently to clarify itself. I experienced a joy then I knew nothing else would ever equal. Not an "I love you" in the world could touch it. Inside that joy I was safe and erotic, excited and at peace, beyond threat or influence. I understood everything I needed to understand in order that I might act, live, be.

Of course I lost it repeatedly. Not only did I lose it, I came to see I was afraid of it. One night at a party in Berkeley I joined a group of people smoking pot. I sat down in the circle and dragged at the joint when it was passed to me. Within seconds I felt the rectangle forming in me, radiating fierce light, shimmering and moving about, not clear and steady as usual. Another minute and the walls began to come together. I knew that when the walls met the breath in my body would be snuffed out, and I would die. I sat there in a roomful of friends and acquaintances, with Stefan there as well, and I said calmly to myself, "You're all alone. They don't understand. There's no way to make them understand. In a few minutes you'll be dead, and none of them can help you. You're alone in this, perfectly alone." I couldn't speak, I could barely breathe. Just as the walls were about to meet, panic forced me to my feet. "I'm ill," I announced loudly, "I'm terribly ill. Oh, God, I'm so ill! Help me. I'm ill." Stefan guided me home, speaking softly to me all the way. I didn't smoke pot again for years.

Stefan knew more about work than I did but not, I think, much more. He was tormented by the discrepancy between his painterly ideas and his ability to execute those ideas on the canvas, and he dramatized his torment endlessly. He would crash about in the studio, smoking, cursing, throwing paint on the canvas, but not, I suspect, thinking hard about the problem before him. The knowledge that work is patient, sustained labor—no more, no less—was not a wisdom he had as yet taken in very much better than I had.

One night he stood for a long time in front of three paintings. Then he began kicking them to pieces. "Shit!" he yelled at them. "All shit!" And he slammed out the door. At two in the morning the doorbell sounded. There was Stefan, half dead, in the arms of a painter friend of his. He reeked of vomit and shit, his eyes were closed, his body sagged, pulling his friend down with him. "Goddammit, Stefan!" the painter shouted. "Stand up!" The friend looked at me, rolled his eyes to the ceiling, and said, "He got polluted so fast I never even saw it coming. Suddenly he's out of the bar and running up the street whooping like an Indian. I tried to stop him, but he's so quick when he gets like this. He ran up to two men and a woman on the street. Before I could stop him, he had lifted the woman's dress and bitten her ass. Those guys were out to destroy him. But then I got there . . ."

I looked at Stefan falling to the floor in our hallway, and I thought, Who is this man? What am I doing here? I don't think I ever stopped thinking, What am I doing here? He got drunk and I got depressed. He smoldered and I disapproved. He slashed at his paintings and I felt scorn and amazement.

Once, when the tension between us had been building for a week, Stefan came into the study where I sat pretending to read. He dropped to his knees and wrapped his arms around my legs. I looked down at him, he up at me. "Well?" he said softly. "How long this time?" I put out my hand and pushed back the hair on his forehead. He took my hand and kissed the palm. I rose. We moved in a despairing embrace into the bedroom. I saw Nettie's face in the air before me, shaking itself back and forth in a motion of disavowal. This is not what I had in mind for you, she was saying. Stefan and I lay down on the bed. "Love me!" he whispered. I pressed myself against him, held him close. "I do, I do," I whispered back. And it was true: as true as I could make it. I did love him, I did. But only down to a certain point. Beyond that point, something opaque in me, there was no give. I could see the opacity. I could taste it and touch it. Between me and my feeling for Stefan, perhaps for any man, I wasn't sure, there fell a kind of transparent membrane through which I could whisper "I do" and make the whisper heard but not felt. Nettie hovered in the air. Her image was quick to the touch, warm and alive. I was right up against it, no obstructions, no interference. The thing was, I could imagine her. She was real to me, he was not.

We lived together five years. Then one day Stefan left the house and he didn't come back. Our marriage was ended. And indeed, why not? We had each wearied of the struggle between us. We each wanted to take a breath in rooms free of that oppressive tension. We wanted that more than we wanted to be together. I dismantled the flat, sold everything in it, left graduate school (always an abstraction to me), and returned to New York. I was thirty years old, and I was relieved to be alone. I moved into the little tenement apartment on First Avenue and got myself a job writing for a weekly newspaper. I fixed up the apartment. In no time at all the place was cozy. The colors all worked this time: no surprises between the can and the wall. I had a desk built that was just right for me: high enough, slim enough, manageable enough. I worked during the day, and in the evening I lay down on the couch to read. Often, however, I lost the concentration for reading rather quickly, and then I'd find myself lying there for hours on end, staring into space.

These were years when women like myself were being called New, Liberated, Odd (myself I preferred Odd, I still do), and indeed, I was new, liberated, odd during the day when I sat at the desk, but at night when I lay on the couch staring into space my mother materialized in the air before me, as if to say, "Not so fast, my dear. All is not done between us."

We are on Delancey Street, walking toward the Williamsburg Bridge. My mother has surprised me by calling to say, "How about walking across the bridge with me to my old neighborhood?" (Her family had moved to Brooklyn a

155

few years before she met my father and Williamsburg had been her last neighborhood as an unmarried girl.)

"But, Ma," I say, "you hate the Lower East Side. You're always refusing to cross Houston Street." (When relatives from Israel want to go to Orchard Street she takes them down to Houston, points across six lanes of traffic, and leaves. "I've had enough of Orchard Street," she tells them.)

"Well, to walk across the bridge, I'll manage the East Side somehow. Besides, I haven't been on Delancey Street in thirty years. I'm curious."

As we cross the crowded, filthy, immigrant street, now black and Puerto Rican instead of Jewish and Italian, she marvels at how changed it all is. I tell her nothing has changed, only the color of the people and the language spoken. The hungry, angling busy-ness of Delancey Street—the cheap clothing stores, the jumbled shoe carts, the linens at discount and the furniture on installment, the thousand hole-in-corner shops selling candy and razor blades, shoelaces and cigarettes, flashlights and clotheslines—is all still in place.

We near Essex Street and my mother says, "Remember the Levinsons? I wonder if the store is still here."

Remember the Levinsons!

"Of course I remember the Levinsons," I say. "Yes, I think the store is still here."

"Do any of the boys work in the store? The youngest one—Davey, was it?—if I remember, he refused. You knew him later, didn't you?"

"Yes, he refused. Yes, I knew him."

"Do you ever see him anymore?"

Ten years ago on Fourteenth Street a solidly built, half-

156

bald man wearing a shapeless tweed coat, with soft dark hair curling around a high naked forehead, and dark eyes narrowed behind black-framed glasses, said hesitantly to me, "Is that you?" I stopped and looked hard at the stranger.

"Davey," I said. "Davey Levinson."

He smiled at me. "What're ya doin' now?"

"I'm a journalist, Davey. I work for newspapers and magazines."

He peered at me. I was sure he hadn't understood journalist or newspaper. Then he said, "You like Baudelaire?" and he took Baudelaire out of one tweed pocket. "You like Zen?" he said. "I got Zen, too." He removed Zen from the other tweed envelope.

Three days later we fell into bed. "There's a lot of things I can't do," Davey said, "but one thing I can do is fuck." He was as good as his word. We went under together, and stayed under for six months.

I shake my head no, I don't see Davey anymore.

"What a bunch they were," my mother laughs as we near the old Levinson clothing store on Essex at the corner of Delancey. "Remember them all? The four boys and Dorothy? And her, the mother? 'Levinson,' I used to say to her, 'take the enema bag off the table before your husband comes home, and the shoes, too.' But she wouldn't listen to me. She'd only cry because he didn't love her. And he? Jake Levinson? He slept with every woman who walked into the store. He never came up to the country to see them the whole summer. Maybe one weekend he came. She'd stand in the kitchen, always in that wet housedress, and cry and cry because he didn't love her and the children called her imbecile.

"She was so beautiful, poor thing," my mother says, walking through the blare and garbage of Delancey Street. "Dark and lovely, just like the children. But fat. Oy, was she fat. Remember how fat she was? And she got fatter as the years went on. I came to see her once, here, right here"—she points down Essex Street—"in the apartment above the store. Remember? You came with me. I thought, She's filling up the room. How will she get out, or back in? But good-natured? None more good-natured than she. When you were sick, and I was falling away from exhaustion, she sat up all night with you, putting mustard plasters on your chest. Remember? It was terrible! All she wanted was Jake, and all she got was sitting up nights with sick children."

Mrs. Levinson sat up with the children for the rest of her life, and worse, infinitely worse, the children sat up with her. They yelled and screamed, pounded their fists, flung themselves at sex and drugs, night school and marriage, and not one of them left Essex Street. When Davey and I met up again he had a sixteen-year-old son. He had gotten a girl in the neighborhood pregnant ("I fucked her on the kitchen sink while her parents were listening to the Yiddish radio station in the next room"), and at nineteen he had been a husband and a father, living down the block from his parents. (Davey on family life: "When my son was an infant my wife put him on the bed without any protection. I told her to put pillows around him. She wouldn't. One night we were watching TV and I heard from the other room a thud to remember for the rest of my life. I went in and he was laying on the floor like an overturned cockroach, stunned. I went back in the living room. I gave her a shot in the mouth I think she can feel it to this day.")

We're nearing the approach to the Williamsburg Bridge. "There's so much traffic!" my mother cries. "How do we get onto the bridge? I'm confused." I'm confused myself, the walkway *is* hard to find. I turn and turn, wheeling amid gas fumes and hamburger grease, rock radio and screaming mothers. Suddenly Delancey Street is overpowering. The frantic accumulation, the noise, the urgency are an oppression. I stand there, feeling ill, and I am remembering how loving Davey had become, finally, oppressive in much the same way: all noise and frenzy, a tumult of poverty and helplessness.

When Davey and I were together we went back one summer afternoon to Ben's Bungalows. The place was sad, silent, dusty, long fallen into disuse and disrepair. On the bus Davey had become moody. "I would say that I've had an unhappy life," he said. "Not only because of what my life has actually been, but because of what life *is*. I'm disappointed. Not only because I don't have the creative powers I want. I'm disappointed because the trees don't talk to me, or the grass or the flowers. I'm disappointed because the flies mistake me for a piece of horseshit." And when we got to Ben's, and were tramping about the deserted grounds, he said, "I'm glad we came back here. I'm glad that we came and saw the place abandoned, and destroyed, and the brambles growing over everything. Because that's the *truth*. I'm glad we came and saw the truth. If we hadn't we might have always thought that it was just *us*. That it was just that we didn't make it but somehow all the others did. That it was just us that missed our connection somehow, didn't take the right road, or make the right move."

Davey always said "us" to me, as though our lives and our destinies were one, and I guess as long as I was sleeping with him he had the right to consider me an honorary Levinson. But I kicked and thrashed against that "us," and we ended in despair.

When I met him on Fourteenth Street Davey was a social worker, living in the Grand Street housing project and working in the Chinatown welfare office. He did nothing but go to his job and read. He read on the subway going to work, at his desk during his lunch hour, and after supper on his bed, a huge mahogany bedstead propped against the wall of an otherwise empty room. He read Thomas Mann and Herman Wouk, Bernard Malamud and Rod McKuen, Dylan Thomas and Philip Wylie, Marcel Proust and Alan Watts. For Davey, reading was a laser beam—narrow, focused, intent—driving into a vast darkness. In his late twenties, after he had left his wife and son, he discovered therapy, and psychoanalysis became the great drama of his life. He absorbed its language and its insights in much the same way that he read great literature: he grew wise in a vacuum.

He would announce, "Anger is fear," and observe in three admirably concise paragraphs why this elegant cliché remained worthy of our attention. He would deliver epigrammatic bits of wisdom: "People are like pool balls after the cue ball has shot into them, rolling every which way, continually hitting each other, knocking each other out of the way, full of greed, envy, violence, jealousy." And he would give me moral instruction: "You must observe with-

160

out blame or praise, acceptance or rejection." These delights of the mind never seemed to go anywhere, or to be seriously related in a way that mattered. His intelligence was like a piece of railroad track severed at either end from the main connection, with a single train car riding it back and forth between stations, imitating motion and journey.

Meanwhile, I couldn't believe I was sleeping with Davey Levinson. Every time we went to bed I felt both twelve and thirty-five. I hungered for him, burrowed into him, couldn't get enough of him. I gave without stint and took without stint. We made love around the clock, ate Chinese food at three in the morning, and played the New Yorker's game of mutual analysis. Later I began to buck and withdraw, turn on him like a snake, be amazed and outraged to find myself there with him (*how did I get back here, how did I get back here*), but for many months whatever we said and did delighted me.

Davey was a recapitulation of my history with men—when I considered him powerful I'd been a clumsy belligerent; when I saw he was weak I became a desirous woman—except that with Davey, for the first time, I saw the configuration whole. I saw my bondage, and I was shamed by my release. How angry and scared I became when I had clear sight! And how pained that it was through Davey I had achieved it. Because I knew Davey. I could imagine him right through to the center. I loved his appetite and I recognized his fears: they were my own. I knew how Davey had gotten to be the way he was, and in his presence I knew better how I had gotten to be the way I was. For a time this openly shared knowledge made us friends. There was between us a mute tenderness for our

161

common beginning. The way we slept was emblematic of our relationship: we lay curled around ourselves facing each other.

One Monday morning, as he was leaving, Davey said, "I hope your week will be productive, constructive, and creative." I nodded, flung my arms around him, buried my lips in his neck, and murmured, "Without greed, violence, envy, or jealousy." His cheeks reddened, he laughed and hugged me closer. But the day was coming when he wouldn't laugh, and certainly he would not draw me closer.

I had confided my fears and insecurities to him. He took them seriously, as a lover is required to do. He did not take seriously what they signified. I was often away on assignment, he was always waiting for me to come home. It began to dawn on him, I think, not only that my struggle with myself over my work was long-lasting and that work would repeatedly take me away from him, but that he was not similarly engaged and he had nothing to take *him* away.

When we had been together six months Davey disappeared. I didn't hear from him and I was unable to reach him, either by phone or by mail. Two weeks passed. Then I called one day and he answered the phone. I said hello, and he began speaking in tongues. A strange psychospiritual-metaphysical babble seemed to have taken possession of him. I kept saying, "What are you talking about?" Finally, in a loud, clear voice, he said, "You must exorcise your father's spirit. Your masculine-feminine natures are pulling at each other. You are not a whole woman. I can only marry a whole woman."

I received this information in silence. Then I said, "Well . . . in the meantime . . . can't we just fuck?"

The following Saturday we spent an exhausting, obsessed twenty-four hours together. We made love continuously, and he talked endlessly at me. Over and over again he said to me, "I am the universe. You must spread your legs wide, open your womb to me. In me will be united all that you are, all poetry, kindness, tenderness, aggressiveness, all that is vibrant, glowing, alive, beautiful in the universe. If you marry me your children will all be virile, robust, poets, makers of music, full of majesty. If you don't they will be faggots and lesbians, evil and diseased." He crooned, hissed, and spat at me. We left the house once to go to a movie. Sitting in the dark, in relation to nothing that was happening on the screen, he gripped my arm and whispered in my ear, "The masculine and the feminine are one. You will not let them be one. In you is both the masculine and the feminine, the light and the dark, the black and the void. Let them come together and you will be one, you will be whole, you will be all, the woman and the man, the universal human."

On Tuesday of the following week I left New York on a journalistic assignment. An hour before I was to go, Davey called.

"Don't respond," he hissed at me. "Simply listen to what I say. Let it all flow through your mind as I've taught you. Let it flow through, right through. Then you will think about it."

I coughed.

"Don't respond, I say!"

Silence. Long silence. Then: "Your father was a witch, he bewitched you, left you guilty, that's why you feel like a shmuck and inferior. That's your true mission as a re-

163

porter. You're traveling around to find your father, or whatever it is he represents. When you find it you'll stop traveling. Take the picture of your father in your bedroom down off the wall. That's the witch in you that keeps it up there. Take it down and turn it to the wall. Take it down. And remember. Talk to no one. Not to your mother or to your friends. No one. Only to God." He stopped speaking. I dared not open my mouth. Then he said, "Goodbye. I love you. When you're ready we'll have babies, and you'll be transformed into the Queen of Israel."

Within a month Davey had made his way to Orthodox Judaism. Overnight he became an eighteenth-century Jew wearing black clothes, sidelocks, and a huge gray-black beard. We met once more. He leaned across the table in a filthy ultra-kosher restaurant on East Broadway to warn me that I must become a good Jewish wife or my soul was lost forever. His breath on my face was hot and sour. At last, I felt his panic and his terrible longing. Within myself, I shrank from him, repelled. This is the last, I thought, absolutely the last.

"There's a policeman," my mother is saying. "Ask him how we get onto the bridge."

We walk over to the cop standing in the middle of the traffic island, cars sweeping past us in all directions.

"How do we get onto the bridge?" I ask.

The cop stares at me. "Why?" he asks.

"We'd like to walk across it."

"You're kidding me."

"No, I'm not. Why?"

"Lady, every week three to seven people get mugged on

this bridge. What chance do you think you two will have? I definitely recommend you forget the whole thing."

"So," my mother says dully. "Nothing's changed on Delancey Street, has it?"

"Come on, Ma. We'll take the subway."

I sat at the desk and I struggled to think. That's how I liked to put it. For years I said, "I'm struggling to think." Just as my mother said she was struggling to live. Mama thought she deserved a medal for swinging her legs over the side of the bed in the morning, and I guess I did, too, just for sitting at the desk.

In the little tenement apartment on First Avenue the fog came rolling in the window. Vapor thickened the air, and mist filled the room. I sat with my eyelids nailed open against the fog, the vapor, the mist, straining to see through to my thoughts, trapped inside the murk. Once every few weeks the air cleared for half a second, and quick! I'd get down two paragraphs of readable prose. Time passed. Much time. Much dead time. Finally, a page. Then two pages. When there were ten pages I rushed to print. I looked at my paragraphs in print: really looked at them. How small, I thought. How small it all is. I've been sitting here so long with these pages, and they're so small. A man said to me, "Good insight. Pity you didn't have time to develop it." A woman said, "What you could do if you didn't have to meet journalistic deadlines. A shame there's no government subsidy." I started to speak. Misery dissolved in my mouth, glued my lips shut. What would I say if I could speak? And to whom would I say it?

I "struggled" on.

Two years after I left Davey Levinson sitting in the restaurant on East Broadway I interviewed Joe Durbin for a story I was writing on a rent strike. He was a labor organizer on the left, and a throwback to the romantic figures of my earliest life. The union movement was Joe's passion. He had been an official in the CIO, known every labor leader from John L. Lewis to Walter Reuther, and had organized all over the historical map: California in the thirties, Michigan in the forties, New York in the fifties. He was twenty years older than me, and he was married. The age difference gave me my control. A week after the interview he called to suggest dinner. We were together six years.

The connection was immediate and primary. Without discussion or analysis we moved directly into the heart of the feeling. In a single fluid motion we had achieved both peace and excitement. "Home," my body said to me, "I'm home."

I did not think to ask what Joe's body was saying to him; it seemed unnecessary. He visited me nearly every day, called when he said he'd call, came when he said he'd come. He was, I knew, even more devoted than I to maintaining the swiftly moving current of infatuation. Insecurity was not going to slow us down. Joe was as good an organizer in love as in politics: next to the labor movement he most adored women. That is, he adored feeling alive through the act of love, and was possessed of great tenderness for the agent of renewed vitality.

I realized it was not me he was adoring, I knew it was the hungriness that had awakened in him, yet I lay back on the bed smiling secretly to myself, exactly as though what I knew to be true wasn't true at all. You would have thought I was Nettie. "It's not me he loves," I said to myself as he bent over me, "it's the sensation I arouse in him"—and then didn't believe what I told myself at all. I couldn't. No one under the influence can. And in some ways it was not so farfetched that I not believe myself. With Joe I was learning better something I already knew: that sex buys time. I saw that whenever we went to bed we were drawn into an exchange of feeling that repeatedly took us by surprise. The surprise kept us coming back for more. Thus, we remained locked in an embrace that caused each of us to look on occasion into the face of the other.

He had a million war stories and he never stopped telling them. A tall noisy man whose voice dominated the room, Joe was endlessly absorbed by his own effort to make sense of things. I think each time he told one of his old stories he expected to find something new in it that would explain things better than it had the time before. In his late fifties, the man did not know the meaning of mental repose. Engagement was the need of his soul: he responded to everything. If the terms of an argument were foreign to him, or the circumstance he found himself in confusing, or a set of gestures unintelligible, he rapidly translated the terms, puzzled out the circumstance, made an interpretation that persuaded him he understood what

167

was going on. He found it unbearable to live in a world he could not make sense of. If he couldn't make sense of things he couldn't act, and to act was his necessity.

In this respect we were wonderfully matched. I had been uncertain all my life about how to act, but I, too, could not live a minute an hour a day except in a state of indiscriminate verbal responsiveness: I had a position on everything. What's more, my anxiety over an absence of response in others was monumental. In the face of silence I talked rapidly and at overwhelming length to fill what I experienced as the void, exhausting myself and those who had brought down on me the punishing need to speak words, words, words. With Joe it was heaven. We had a built-in mechanism for release and replenishment. We talked ourselves to a frenzy, then made fierce and dreamy love, then uncoupled and went on talking.

Our exchange was not exactly conversation. Carried on at a high level of speed and noise, it consisted of a series of rapid-motion confrontations. Assertion, denial, defense was the way we understood talking. And the more urgent the facedown—that is, the more volatile and explosive— the more stimulated and reassured, I think, each of us was. This appetite we had for arguing the point right down to the ground was a measure of how fundamental a weapon we both conceived the articulating intelligence to be. If we could each persuade the other to see the truth as we saw it, the world would somehow turn on its axis and all that thwarted us would be emptied out into harmless space.

We paid no real attention to the fact that we quarreled continuously. We laughed about what a social cliché we were: the feminist and the leftist locked together in erotic

168

battle. We thought because we were always talking we were connecting. In truth, we connected only in bed. On our feet we defended positions. Given such tumult, it seems remarkable now that the surprises kept coming.

One day, when we had been together six or eight months, we went for a walk and met a school friend of mine. She suggested a cup of coffee. Joe, thinking to be socially responsible and to charm my friend, took over the conversation. That is, he did not allow conversation to develop. If one of us said, "There's a banana peel on the sidewalk," Joe said, "Speaking of banana peels, that reminds me of the time in Flint, Michigan, when . . ." and he was off on a twenty-minute labor story. My friend looked puzzled. Joe did not notice. In a few minutes he repeated the performance. If we had been alone I would have exploded at him. As it was, I kept my mouth shut and watched. I began to see him through my friend's eyes. I heard him as I thought she heard him. I imagined her thinking: Here's an overbearing blusterer one doesn't engage with, one simply walks away from, too exhausting to try to make terms here.

Suddenly I felt lonely, terribly lonely. "Let's go back to the house," I said when we had parted from my friend, "I don't feel well." Joe put his hand up for a cab. Once inside the apartment I tore my clothes off and dragged him into bed.

"I thought you don't feel well," he said.

"I'll feel better if we make love," I explained.

But I didn't. I still felt lonely. Joe didn't notice. He was propped against the pillows, his legs extended on the bed, chattering on, adding to the Flint, Michigan, story, caressing me steadily, mindlessly, as he spoke. I lay against his chest feeling more and more isolated.

"Oh, stop!" I cried. "Please stop. Stop!"

Joe's mouth closed in the middle of a sentence. His head pulled back. His eyes searched mine. "What is it, darling?" he said. He'd never heard me sound this note before.

"Listen to me," I pleaded, "just listen to me." He nodded at me, not taking his eyes from mine. "You don't know me at all," I said. "You think I'm this hot-shot loud-mouthed liberated woman, as brash and self-confident as you, ready to walk across the world just like you, and that's not who I am at all. It's making me lonely now to make love with you, and you not know what my life is about." He nodded again.

I told him then how I had hungered for a life like his but that I hadn't ever had it, that I'd always felt marginal, buried alive in obscurity, and that all the talk I manufactured couldn't dissolve out the isolation. I told him how sometimes I wake spontaneously in the night and I sit up in bed and I'm alone in the middle of the world. "Where *is* everybody?" I say out loud, and I have to calm myself with "Mama's in Chelsea, Marilyn's on Seventy-third Street, my brother's in Baltimore." The list, I told him, is pathetic.

I talked and talked. On and on I went, without pause or interruption. When I stopped I felt relieved (alone now but not lonely) and, very quickly, embarrassed. He was so silent. Oh, I thought, what a fool you are to have said these things. He doesn't like any of this, not a bit of it, he doesn't even know what you're talking about. Then Joe

170

said, "Darling, what a rich inner life you have." My eyes widened. I took in the words. I laughed with delight. That he had such a sentence in him! That he had spoken the sentence he had in him. I loved him then. For the first time I loved *him*.

"What about his wife," my mother said. "What about you," my friends said. I ran into an acquaintance on the street. She wore silver earrings and curly gray hair, her eyes danced with interest, her smile was warm and knowing. "You'll need a lot of stamina and a lot of self-control," she said. This woman understood the issues better.

It was assumed by everyone I knew that Joe's wife was the wife, and I the other woman, and Joe the prize slated to fall to one or the other of us, but such was not the case. Why, I thought, would I want him to leave his wife? What would I do then? Take him into my apartment? It's too small. Besides, I may not like sleeping alone, but I like waking up alone. Yes, it's painful when he leaves, but it's not that painful. The situation suits me. And then again, it's interesting.

Joe's wife was an abstraction to me. I felt neither guilt nor jealousy toward her. This because I did not feel jealous of Joe, whose gifts for life (gifts he made use of in union organizing as well as in love affairs) included thoroughgoing reliability and a remarkable constancy of mood. A man of immense appetite and energy, Joe had quality time for all. When he was there he was so thoroughly and unreservedly there I felt neither deprived nor possessive when

171

he wasn't. For the first time, what a lover did when he was not with me was of no real concern; in fact, it was none of my business. This *was* an experience.

Imagine. I was living entirely in the moment, with no formal assurance beyond tomorrow morning's telephone call, and I found myself interested; not sad tearful frightened or resentful, only interested. Here, I reasoned, is a circumstance where you clearly cannot make terms. The truth is, one never makes terms. This affair is only the bare, unfiltered truth. Can you take it in or will you founder on the absence of illusion? Indeed, it was stamina and self-control that were required to answer the question. I rose to the task. I began to grasp the idea of living without a future: we had few moments to waste on bad behavior. I saw errant impulses die before they could make trouble. I saw reflexive anger give way to analytic understanding. I saw petty indulgence stifle itself and a kind of rough emotional justice prevail. All this I saw, and all this I was pleased to see. Then a day came when I also saw that learning to live without a future is a sterile exercise: what looks like life within a walled garden is really life inside a renovated prison yard. Joe's wife remained an abstraction, but Joe's marriage became a stunning confinement.

We occupied a universe composed of one room in one season: my bedroom on weekday afternoons. As time went on, we occupied this universe more and more fully. Hunger multiplied on hunger, desire on desire. We couldn't get enough. Because we didn't get enough. I was always wanting more. "Not more," a friend said evenly. "Enough. You want enough." In a year or two I realized that it wasn't exactly more I wanted, or even enough. It was a larger world for our feelings to walk about in. Life requires space as well as air and light, room for exploration and self-discovery. The limits of exploration on the life of our feelings were set by Joe's marriage, and those limits were close in. However deeply we might feel, our love could not make laws or map territory. There was no country of experience for it to cross, no coast to reach, no center to penetrate. We were in possession of a small interior space somewhere in the midst of a fertile region of unknown proportion. Around this space stood boundaries of rigid stability. Love might intensify, but it could never expand to occupy a territory made in its own shape. The reality of the predetermined limit bit into me.

At about this same time I realized that the rectangle inside of which my thoughts lived or died was also a small interior space into which my working life had crammed itself, rather than that the work had carved out of the larger body of a free self the shape and extent of the territory it needed to occupy.

For a moment I backed off from myself. I saw that I was suspended inside my own life. Only a small part of it contained substance, I was daydreaming the rest. Joe, and the time I spent at the desk, were equal efforts at manifest destiny. I backed off even farther and saw that I could not imagine how I would begin to take possession of the larger territory, either in love or in work.

So then, in my late thirties I led a fantasy life in work and in love: rich, dreamy, girlish, a necessary complement to the impoverished reality. The twin nature of this compul-

173

ive daydreaming led me to a discovery of some consequence.

One week in summer when Joe and I had been together two years I found myself working unusually well. I sat at the desk and I concentrated. I didn't glaze over looking at the words, or stumble about in my chair reeling with fog and fatigue. Rather, I sat down each morning with a clear mind and hour after hour I worked. The rectangle had opened wide and remained open: in the middle stood an idea. A great excitement formed itself around this idea, and took hold of me. I began fantasizing over the idea, rushing ahead of it, envisioning its full and particular strength and power long before it had clarified. Out of this fantasizing came images, and out of the images a wholeness of thought and language that amazed me each time it repeated itself. At the end of the week I had a large amount of manuscript on my desk. On Friday afternoon I put away the work. On Monday morning I looked at it, and I saw that the pages contained merit but the idea was ill-conceived. It didn't work at all. I'd have to abandon all that I had done. I felt deflated. The period of inspired labor was at an end. The murk and the vapor closed in on me again, the rectangle shriveled and I was back to eking out painfully small moments of clarity, as usual and as always. Still, it was absorbing to remember the hours I had put in while under the spell of my vision. I felt strengthened by the sustained effort of work the fantasizing had led to.

During this same period of time Joe and I achieved a new level of intensity. Every afternoon at four we burned and we drowned. It seemed during those dangerous days as though we were moving toward a climactic moment. In the evening, after he had left me, I would walk in the sweet hours of final daylight, fantasizing about us. Us together now, us together in the future, us walking, us in bed, us larking about. Us. It came sweeping up in me that week, all nervous excitement, melancholy sweetness, open longing. Then one evening I felt stricken and bereft, frightened to be walking the streets alone, dreaming a life in my head about a man who was off elsewhere, and would always be off elsewhere. I shivered, and felt sick. My stomach ached. I went to bed early that night and woke out of a fitful sleep to find myself once again on the empty landscape. The deep wave of dreamy suggestiveness around which my body had curled all week turned into a bag of worms eating at my insides. Oh, I thought, this is dis-*gust*-ing.

I got up and wrote in my journal: "Love is a function of the passive feeling life, dependent on an ideal other for satisfactory resolution: the primitive position into which we are born. Work is a function of the active expressive life, and if it comes to nothing, one is still left with the strengthening knowledge of the acting self. Only when access to the imaginative life is denied does one go in for love in a big way."

I sat at my desk at four o'clock in the morning looking at the blotter, the bookshelves, the orderly comfort of the place in which I worked, and I thought: Mama worships at the shrine of Love but that lifelong boredom of hers is a dead giveaway.

I went back to bed. In the morning I would struggle on. It was always in the morning I would struggle on. Never right now. Not with work, not with Joe. I could not see that each was a means of escape from the other. With Joe I blissed out, avoided the pure pain of sustained labor. With work I hardened myself against the "intrusion" of love: a married man was just fine. For years I said: In the morning. Which, of course, never came.

Joe was the most socialized man I have ever known. His sense of life was generic: at any given moment any one of twenty-five people could fill the spot for the wife, the lover, the friend. He considered it childish to think human happiness devolved on a particularity of attachment or circumstance. He said the point is to make as much world as possible in whatever small clearing is allotted one. He did not feel the bite of our confinement as I did. Rather he said to himself, "This is what we have to work with, let's see how well we can do with what we've got," and he pitched in.

He never stopped delivering life to me, at me, for me. He was forever creating amenities and pleasures that gave spark and dimension to our exchange. We had champagne in bed, oysters in midtown, surprise trips to the ocean. He brought me books I needed, sent me clippings daily, arranged to stay overnight when I least expected it and made breakfast in the morning. Our emotional life was an absorbing subject for me, and became one for him as well. He delighted in the extensive nature of the discussion, entered into it without fear or defensiveness, and soon had me hooked on the regular feeding such talk provided me with.

I watched with tender amusement as he bent over backward not only to be reliable and loving each day but also to be continually thinking of how we might have more. Joe never felt he didn't have enough, but he too wanted more and he was always conniving to get it. I didn't think much about the conniving. It seemed natural that I simply let myself be carried along on the wave of bounty it delivered up to both of us.

One day, in the autumn of our third year, Joe told me that a friend of his had a boat he was thinking of buying. The boat was berthed in the Caribbean and Joe was flying down in two weeks to see it. "Come with me," he said. "It'll be great. We'll have two or three days together, maybe longer." I was free, and the proposal came as an unexpected gift. I kissed him all over. What a lovely man, I thought. Always on the lookout.

We flew down to the Caribbean on a Tuesday afternoon. That night we ate dinner on a terrace that hung out over a blue-green bay and made love in a whitewashed room with the night air coming through open shutters, soft and sweet. Bliss. Tuesday night bliss. Wednesday all day bliss. Thursday also bliss. On Friday morning we prepared to leave for New York. We packed up, checked out, and drove our rented car out to the airport. Suddenly I couldn't bear the thought of going back. I laid my hand on Joe's arm and pleaded, "Let's stay over the weekend. Call your wife and tell her you need another day or two for the boat."

Joe turned his head halfway toward me. I saw the frown forming on his forehead, and I saw his eyes narrow. "Sweetie, *I'm* not going back with you," he said. "My wife is coming down this evening."

It was the tone of his voice I never forgot. The slightly puzzled irritation in it. As though he had, of course, already given me this information and he couldn't understand how it was I had forgotten it. I remember afterward thinking: gaslight.

"What?" I said. "What did you say?"

"I said my wife's coming down tonight. I *told* you that. I'm sure I did."

"How dare you," I said. "How the fuck dare you."

He nearly went off the road. Instead, he pulled over and put his head in his hands. I stared out into the bleak tropical morning shimmering with heat and haze.

"I must have forgotten," Joe said. "Forgive me. It was a useful slip of memory, I'm sure. I forgot because I thought it would spoil our time here if you knew."

"That's despicable."

"Why?" he cried. "What's so despicable? I wanted us to have a good time. I didn't think we would if you knew we weren't going back together. So what's so terrible? We *had* a lovely time, didn't we?"

"You manipulated me. You held back information. Decided on your own it was more important we have a good time than that I know everything there was to know. The situation was more important to you than I was."

"That's not true," he said.

But it was true. For Joe, the situation was always more important than anyone in it. Because we spent our lives in the bedroom, I'd not had a chance until now to feel in the flesh what I had long known in the intellect.

My mother was glad I had someone to love. At first she came down on me as hard as she had with Stefan, harder— "So how does it feel to steal another woman's husband?"— but she was quicker now to recover from her confused rages over me and men. As I slammed out the door I heard her calling, "Come back! Come back! I didn't mean that."

And she didn't. Within minutes, it seemed, she had accepted the conditions of our affair and welcomed Joe to her house; was eager, in fact, that he should come. For her, Joe was a glamorous and worldly figure, a man of strength, purpose, and daring. Shivering with coquettish delight, she said admiringly, "The chutzpah of that man!"

She couldn't stop herself from gossiping to the family. When the aunts and uncles asked for me, she said, "Don't ask," in a voice of such juicy insinuation she instantly had their full attention, and then proceeded to inform them that I had become a principal in a tale of high romantic tragedy. The relatives, of course, lost no time in patronizing her with their moral alarm: a married man, a shock and a scandal, no one in the family had ever. Mama got miffed (this wasn't in the script) and announced haughtily that there were aspects of the case she was not free to discuss. They could decide for themselves whether Joe's wife was mad or syphilitic or in a lingering state of something-or-other.

Joe's wife *was* a problem. Once Mama had given her allegiance to us, her conviction that we were victimizing his wife became a source of tormenting conflict. She solved the conflict by dreaming repeatedly that "the wife" stood in my doorway with a gun in her hand, shooting point-blank at me.

179

Mama knew that Joe was a man of appetite and will. She saw the way he dominated conversation, took up more than his share of the room, politicked relentlessly to get what he wanted, but she didn't think it worthwhile to "stand on principle" over this less than attractive character trait. She considered the exertion of will on me small potatoes. Men, she shrugged. What difference did it make. He loves you? He's good to you? So he wants to act like a man. So let him. It does you no harm, it means nothing.

In the fourth year Joe's wife became violently ill with a suddenness that alarmed. It was thought she was going to die. Joe walked around stunned. He had a great affection for his wife, would never leave her while she lived, and feared for her now that she might be dying. Yet his thoughts were confused and his feelings divided. Not a word was spoken about the potential meaning this turn of events held for us, but we were all expectant. Horrified but expectant, and without acknowledging our behavior we began to act as though Joe and I would soon be married.

One afternoon during this time Mama and Sarah dropped by for coffee. The two sisters were always together, and always bickering. Ordinary conversation between them was an entertaining aggression. "A boy fell down in the street," Sarah might say. "The eyes rolled up in the head, the arms and legs going in all directions. First time I saw an epileptic fit." To which Mama would retort, "What are you talking? You know what you're talking? That was a drug addict you saw. You know what means drug addict?" Whereupon Sarah would shake her head. "Your mother. She thinks because onions don't grow on top of her head she's the rabbi's wife." I always enjoyed a visit from the two of them.

At four-thirty Joe barged in. "Sorry," he said, smiling. "Hope I'm not interrupting anything, but I had a piece of good luck this morning, signed a contract we've been fighting over for months. I thought we'd celebrate." He took a bottle of wine out of a paper bag and moved quickly about the room talking nonstop while he arranged four wineglasses on the coffee table, opened the bottle, and poured the wine.

Mama's eyes danced with pleasure. Joe was always a holiday for her. She took the glass from him, and gulped at its liquid content.

"Oh no!" Sarah blushed furiously. "I can't drink wine in the middle of the day."

"Oh yes you can," Joe said, handing her the filled glass. Reluctantly, she took it from him.

Joe and I raised our glasses to each other. Everyone drank. Joe chattered on while Mama and I made appropriate female noises [How wonderful! You didn't *really!* That's fantastic!], but Sarah became very quiet. I felt a twinge to see my voluble aunt so abruptly silenced.

When our glasses were empty Joe raised the bottle again and held it out, first toward me. I extended my glass to meet his raised arm. He poured. He then held the bottle toward Mama. She said, "No more." Sarah waved it away in true alarm. "Ah, come on," said Joe, pushing the bottle at Mama's glass. "Oh well." Mama giggled. He filled her glass, and turned to Sarah. In a firm voice she said, "No, thanks. I don't want any more."

181

"Ah, come on," said Joe, tilting the bottle toward her.

Sarah put her hand over her glass. "No," she said, "I can't."

"So tell me, Joe," Mama said, "how did it go with the bosses this morning?" Joe laughed and began to tell her for the third time, but in a minute or so he turned back to Sarah with the bottle of wine once more in his hand.

"Come *on*," he said.

Sarah was startled, but she placed her hand over her glass again and shook her head. "I really don't want any more," she said.

"Yes you do," Joe said, "you're just shy," and he began to nudge her hand with the mouth of the bottle. "Come on, come on, come on."

Mama looked down at her own glass. Sarah looked painfully confused.

I placed my hand over Joe's. He looked at me. "She's a grown woman," I said. "If she says no, she means no."

For a moment after I'd spoken we remained as we were, my hand over his, our eyes locked. Then Joe withdrew his hand, smiled, and said, "Gotcha." He was a good-natured man, really. He didn't know any other way to be.

At five-thirty the three of them rose to leave. Joe helped Sarah on with her coat, I helped Mama on with hers. I stood in the doorway as they walked to the elevator. Halfway down the corridor Mama stopped. "I left my keys," she called out. When she got back to me I saw that she was holding the keys in her hand. She moved past me into the apartment, looking rattled. "Where could I have left them?" she said, as though speaking to herself.

"Ma, you're holding the keys in your hand."

"Oh, for goodness' sake!" But she stood there looking puzzled. Then she put her hand on my arm. "Don't get married," she said, and fled down the corridor.

Joe's wife did not die. She recovered and we were, after her illness, as we had been before, continuing on in our old explosive way from the fourth year to the fifth to the sixth. Ours was a primitive exchange of energies—the boiling-over talk, the blissed-out lovemaking—that never altered in its character. From time to time, through the noise and smoke, one of us glimpsed the way the other one put the world together and, for a moment, would feel the beating heart at the end of a long line of thought. But the moment was sure to pass. If either of us listened too long to what the other one actually said we found ourselves drifting. That crude energy between us was what we loved. The quarreling turned us on.

At the heart of this noisy, complicated, talk-filled affair, the connection remained erotic. We who talked so passionately together for hours, days, months, and years were sure to lose interest the moment one of us ceased to be aroused in bed. I knew this was the deeper truth between us, I said it out loud—often—and still it was as if I didn't know what the words actually meant. Between the flash of insight and the imperative to act lay miles of anxiety to negotiate.

"Our connection is erotic," I announced periodically.

"Yes?" Joe replied with interest in his voice.

"Neither of us responds to the specific shape or content

183

of the other's mind or spirit. We engage only through sexual arousal."

He laughed and laughed. I had invented the wheel.

"Yes, darling," he said patiently. "That's the way it is between men and women. The connection, as you say, is erotic. So what? What does it mean to characterize us that way?"

"I hate it," I said. "I find it insulting. I have always found it insulting."

"Well, then," he said. "I guess you're just going to have to go on being insulted by a few thousand years of history."

I didn't contradict him then. I subsided instead into a kind of lulled inactivity from which I'd struggle up only briefly when I felt myself pushed out of shape in conversation, or exiled in my thoughts, or generalized in my being ("you women . . ."). Then I'd quiet down again, and for months at a time let it all go. The erotic attachment had its advantages and these, inevitably, weighed in the balance.

To begin with, there was the enormity of sexual love itself. Desire ensured tenderness. Tenderness precluded danger. Once out of danger, I was free to retreat into the absorbing secret life of my own abandon. In bed I didn't have to be myself. I could lose myself, and still I was safe. I'd come out of that lostness and there was Joe, holding on to me, never more trustworthy than when receiving proof anew of his own vital powers.

I didn't have to be myself. With Joe, for the first time, I felt the allure of not having to be oneself: the sheer relief of it. All my life I had suspected I wasn't interesting enough, special enough, talented enough to hold the attention of those who came toward me in friendship or in love. I could attract people, yes, but could I hold them? I was never sure. Now, it seemed, I didn't have to be sure. The erotic connection brought reprieve. I wasn't under the gun to earn interest or respect daily. The deal was set: I could relax into it. I saw the strong appeal of marriage. To engage as oneself and oneself alone is no longer a requirement: the other half can do the work. Encounters on the open landscape of the world need never imperil one again.

It was interesting, all of it, but deep within myself I turned away. In the sixth year I began to repeat "Our connection is erotic" with monotonous regularity, and always now with a kind of dull anger in my voice. I meant, of course, I wasn't making erotic connection. Our disputes had begun to weary me. Confrontation failed to arouse. I no longer flared with predictable speed or heat. Suddenly we'd have a bad week, wouldn't sleep together. We'd meet then and I'd be sluggish, disoriented. Joe's attention would wander openly. We were trudging uphill, making conversation for an hour and a half.

"We're out of phase just now," one of us said.

"In a dull period," the other confirmed.

"Next week we'll be as we've always been."

And next week we would be as we'd always been: for a day or two.

Bit by bit we were coming unstuck, and we each knew it. The atmosphere was poisoned with confusion and regret. I turned coy: "We can't go on like this forever, you know." Joe turned tough: "Let's quit right now." But on we went.

One night I received a call from my friend Linda. "Everything all right between you and Joe?" she asked.

185

"Sure. Why?"

"He's been calling me."

"What do you mean, he's been calling you?"

"He's been asking to see me. And now I've received a disturbing letter from him."

My heart knocked violently against my chest. "You mean he's making a pass at you?"

"I'm not sure, but I think so."

"That's unbelievable. How could he make a pass at a friend of mine?"

"That's what I thought, but the letter is so provocative I felt I should let you know."

"Yes, of course. Thanks, thanks for calling."

Linda was a labor reporter Joe had met often in my house. Perhaps his calls had something do with work. Yes, that must be it. It was something to do with his work. He was bound to mention it to me this week.

But he didn't mention it that week, or the week after. In the interim I'd met Linda and seen the letter: it was an open invitation to an affair.

I told Joe that Linda had called and that I'd seen his letter. He was astonished. "She called you? I can't believe it. What kind of friend is that?"

"A good friend, that's what kind."

"Not in my book."

"You mean she should have kept quiet?"

"I mean just that."

"Not that you shouldn't have made a pass at her, but that she should have kept quiet about it, is that it?"

"Oh no you don't. I'm not going to defend myself, and that's that. I haven't felt guilty toward my wife all these

186

years, and I don't feel guilty toward you. You and I have been falling to pieces for a long time now. As far as sex goes, I consider myself a free agent."

"But why a friend of mine? Can't you see that's out of bounds."

"Not at all. Who else is one attracted to but the friends of one's friends? My being attracted to Linda is not a sin; her telling you is. I don't see why a friend would want to tell you something that might hurt you."

I stared at him. He really didn't see why.

"If Linda keeps silent," I said, "the two of you share a secret. I immediately lose equal standing. I become the deceived wife. That's the one without all the information. How could you so misread Linda as to think she'd do that to me? For what? A roll in the hay?"

"Bullshit. That's not the way I see it at all. If she didn't want to make it, fine. She keeps her mouth shut and we all go on as before. I've made passes at my friends' wives all my life, and yes, at the friends of my own wife. In no instance did a wife run to tell her husband, or a friend run to tell my wife. It's malicious nonsense to think 'honesty' is being invoked when a phone call is made to announce adulterous intentions."

"You say that because you've lived your life among married people for whom marriage is paramount. The humiliations endured by the women and men inside the marriage are less important to all of you than the marriage itself. It's so unfriendly! Why would Linda or I share such a value? What world do you think we're living in?"

"I don't know what the hell you're talking about. This happens every day of the week, every hour on the hour.

187

It's the way of the world, the most fundamental of drives, it has nothing to do with friendship."

"I guess that's it," I said slowly. "We've come to the heart of it. I think it distinctly *un*friendly of you to make a pass at a friend of mine, but you feel fine about it, because you think love has nothing to do with friendship."

"You're such a fool," Joe said softly. "With all you know, you still don't know it's an adversarial relation. There is no friendship in love."

"I refuse that definition," I said. "I absolutely refuse it. If love is only romantic attachment, fuck it."

"You're a child," Joe said. "That's what love *is*. There's no other way to have it."

"Then I'll do without," I said. "This way I cannot live." He made no reply then. We faced each other across a long silent moment.

"I guess it was inevitable," I said, "that I, too, would become the deceived wife."

"Somebody always is," Joe said. "Sometimes it's even me."

And quite suddenly we had come to the end.

I wanted to put on my sneakers and take a walk across the world, from the Battery to the George Washington Bridge, but a sledgehammer of fatigue forced me down onto the couch where I lay staring into space. I felt real despair then. However much I sought to differentiate myself, I seemed always to end up like Mama, lying on the couch staring into space. And never more so than when I saw that sleeping with Joe *had* been like sleeping with my father, not because he was older and married, but because he was a man whose view of life made inevitable the equation man-husband-papa, woman-wife-child.

I went reeling back over my life with men: Stefan, Davey, Joe. They had seemed so different, one from another, but I'd learned nothing from these attachments, I'd been hiding out with all of them. It was almost as though I chose men who would ensure I'd arrive back at this moment, depressed and paralyzed by the failure of love.

After a while I got up off the couch. I didn't take a hike across the world—so far from touching firm ground, I felt myself adrift in a shipwrecked sea—but I did sit down at the desk. I clung to the daily effort: I couldn't do *it* very well, either, but I never doubted the desk—not the satisfactory resolution of love—was the potential lifesaver.

I walked into an analyst's office. I told her everything. I told her everything again. And then again. Whenever I told her everything she said: Why?

Why? I repeated blankly.

Yes, why, she replied calmly.

She was always saying why to me. Why all this breathlessness. Why just this rectangle. Why only a small interior space always under attack. Why does the space not enlarge and expand to fill your life. Why.

As the whys fell on me I was running, running through the streets of the city, the streets of my life. I sat chained to the desk, running. Breathless, exhausted, frantic. Sketch it in! Sketch it in! No time, no breath. Maybe someday there'll be breath and time, right now just get the bare bones of the thing down. The rectangle is closing in. Work fast, faster. I can't. There's a pain in my side. I can barely sit at the typewriter. I feel ill, I'm about to faint, hanging on, another half hour at the typewriter and I'll fall to the ground. I'd better chain myself to the typewriter, otherwise . . .

Why, she asked. Why chained to the typewriter. Why fighting for time and breath. Why only that small bit of good writing inside a narrow space, and all around the rhetoric of panic and breathlessness.

That rectangle, I finally explained. It's a fugitive, a subversive, an illegal immigrant in the country of my being. It has no civil rights. It's always on the run.

"How about a woman with a husband?" she asked. "Is she the native citizen? The one with all the rights?"

"I think . . . maybe yes . . . perhaps yes." And I was surprised by the sadness in my voice. "You may be right. That may be it."

"Well, then, let's get you married," she said briskly. "Nothing easier than that."

"No!" I cried hotly. "No, no, no. A thousand times no."

"Well, then," she said.

"I can't seem to do it." I hit the palm of one hand with the fist of the other. "I can't naturalize the immigrant."

Again she said why.

And this time when she said why I saw myself standing in the foyer with Mama and Nettie, the pale light full of

190

threat and anxiety falling on us. That foyer. It is an essence, a kind of perfumed ether. I breathe it in. It thrills and sedates me. I stand in the foyer, aroused and attentive, suspended and immobilized.

Why, she said. I want to know why. Why will you not leave that dark narrow passage?

My mother materialized in the air, her face soft, weak, sadly intelligent. She leaned forward intently. She was as interested in the question as I. But I remained mute. I had no answer.

Then the analyst said, What about men?

Men? I repeated blankly.

Yes, men, she said calmly.

Oh, for God's sake! I exploded. I can't do that one, *too!* I spoke more slowly then. I realized only as I spoke that what I had said was true. No, I said quietly, I don't think I can learn to do that one.

You must, she said even more quietly. You must do work, and you must do love.

Mama and Nettie held me in a loose embrace. Yes, they smiled, wreathing their arms about me in the pale light, you must.

The years are coming up thickly . . . forty-six, forty-seven, forty-eight . . . There is no past now, only the ongoing present . . . seventy-eight, seventy-nine, eighty. Eighty. My God, my mother is eighty. We stand still, looking at

191

each other. She shrugs her shoulder and sits down on the couch in her living room.

She came to my house this afternoon. We had a drink, then went out to dinner in the neighborhood, then I walked her home. She made coffee and we talked, looked at pictures, some old (America, 1941), some older (Russia, 1913), and we read together from a batch of letters we have dipped into fifty times in my life; letters written to her in 1922 by one Noah Shecter, formerly a professor of literature in Rumania and at the time of the letter-writing manager of the bakery where my mother worked as a bookkeeper. The letters are remarkable: nineteenth-century romantic fantasy written by a lonely man living in the Bronx with an un-intellectual wife and three needy children, his head filled with Ibsen, Gorki, Mozart, writing his heart out each night at midnight to a vain brown-eyed empty vessel of receptivity (my eighteen-year-old mother) who would read these impassioned outpourings at eight in the morning before she went off to work to see the man who had written them stiff and formal in a high starched collar, looking like Franz Kafka in the insurance company. Now, sixty years later, I hold these hundreds of yellowed sheets covered with thickly scrawled European handwriting, the black ink long ago turned brown, and read of Noah Shecter's midnight desperation that my mother should understand how full his heart is, just having seen Ibsen's *Brand* performed in a Fourteenth Street theater, and how necessary it is that he let her know how well the actors captured the essential meaning of this very great play. The letters and the pictures surround us (I see her as she must have looked when she first read them)—fragments, scraps, tales told and retold of the life lived and the life unlived. Especially the one unlived.

A sad, silent weight hangs about my mother all evening. She looks very pretty tonight—soft white hair, soft smooth skin, the wrecked face looking wonderfully whole again— but the years are dragging inside her, and in her eyes I see the confusion, the persistent confusion.

"A lifetime gone by," she says quietly.

My pain is so great I dare not feel it. "Exactly," I say evenly. "Not lived. Just gone by."

The softness in her face hardens into definition. She looks at me and, with iron in her voice, says in Yiddish, "So you'll write down: From the beginning it was all lost."

We sit together then, silent, not embroiled with each other, two women only staring into the obscurity of all that lost life. My mother looks neither young nor old, only deeply absorbed by the terribleness of what she is seeing. I do not know how I look to her.

We always walked, she and I. We don't always walk now. We don't always argue, either. We don't always do any of the things we always did. There is no always anymore. The fixed patterns are beginning to break up. This breakup has its own pleasures and surprises. In fact, surprise is now the key word between us. We cannot depend on change, but we can depend on surprise. However, we cannot always depend on surprise either. This keeps us on our toes.

I come to see her one night with an old friend of mine, a man who grew up with me, someone we've both known for thirty years. I say known advisedly. This man is something of a lunatic. An inspired lunatic, to be sure, but a lunatic nonetheless. He, like Davey Levinson, is educated in a vacuum, and he speaks a kind of imaginative gibberish. It is the only way he knows how to get through the ordinary anxiety of the ordinary day.

We are having coffee and cake. I am eating too much cake. I am, in fact, wolfing down the cake. My mother is getting crazy watching me. She cries, "Stop it! For God's sake, stop eating like that. Don't you care at all that you'll gain two pounds and hate yourself tomorrow? Where's your motivation?"

My friend, sitting at the table beside me, his head thrust forward and down and twisted to the side, looking at her like the madman that he is, starts going on nonsensically about motivation. "You know, of course, that motivation is life," he says. "Life itself. Taken from the Latin *motus*, it means to move, set in motion, engage . . ."

My mother looks at him. I can see in her face that she does not understand the construction of these sentences. She feels put down: if she doesn't understand something she is being told she is stupid. Her expression becomes one of glittering scorn. "You think you're telling me something I don't know?" she says. "You think I was born yesterday?" No surprise here.

One week later I'm sitting in her apartment drinking tea with her, and from out of nowhere she says to me, "So tell me about your abortion." She knows I had an abortion when I was thirty, but she has never referred to it. I, in

194

turn, know she had three abortions during the Depression, but I never mention them, either. Now, suddenly . . . Her face is unreadable. I don't know what has stirred the inquiry and I don't know what to tell her. Should I tell her the truth or . . . ? What the hell. The truth. "I had an abortion with my legs up against the wall in an apartment on West Eighty-eighth Street, with Demerol injected into my veins by a doctor whose consulting room was the corner of Fifty-eighth Street and Tenth Avenue." She nods at me as I speak, as though these details are familiar, even expected. Then she says, "I had mine in the basement of a Greenwich Village nightclub, for ten dollars, with a doctor who half the time when you woke up you were holding his penis in your hand." I look at her in admiration. She has matched me clause for clause, and raised the ante with each one. We both burst out laughing at the same moment. Surprise.

Yet another night I am sitting at her table and we are talking of the time she went to work when I was eight years old. This is a story I never tire of hearing.

"What made you decide to do it, Ma? I mean, why that time rather than any other?"

"I always wanted to work, always. God, how I loved having my own money in my pocket! It was the middle of the war, you threw a stone you got seven jobs, I couldn't resist."

"So what did you do?"

"I read the want ads one morning and I got dressed, took the subway downtown, and applied for a job. In ten minutes I had it. What was the name of that company? I've forgotten it now."

"Angelica Uniform Company," I instantly supply.

"You remember!" She smiles beatifically at me. "Look at that. She remembers. I can't remember. She remembers."

"I am the repository of your life now, Ma."

"Yes, you are, you are. Let's see now. Where were we?"

"You went downtown and got the job."

"Yes. So I came home and told Papa, 'I have a job.' "

"How did he respond?"

"Badly. Very badly. He didn't want me to work. He said, 'No other wife in the neighborhood works, why should you work.' I said, 'I don't care what any other wife in the neighborhood does, I want to work.' " She stares into this memory, shaking her head. Her voice falters. "But it was no good, no good. I didn't last long."

"Eight months," I say.

"Yes, eight months."

"Why, Ma? Why only eight months?"

"Papa was miserable. He kept saying to me, 'The children need you.' "

"That was silly," I interrupt. "I remember being *excited* that you were working. I loved having a key around my neck, and rushing home every afternoon to do things that made it easier for you."

"Then he said, 'You're losing weight.' "

"You were twenty pounds overweight. It was *great* that you were losing weight."

"What can I tell you?" she says to me. "Either you were going to make a hell in the house or you were going to be happy. I wanted to be happy. He didn't want me to work. I stopped working."

We are quiet together for a while. Then I say, "Ma, if

196

it was now, and Papa said he didn't want you to work, what would you do?"

She looks at me for a long moment. She is eighty years old. Her eyes are dim, her hair is white, her body is frail. She takes a swallow of her tea, puts down the cup, and says calmly, "I'd tell him to go fuck himself."

Real surprise.

We're in the Lincoln Center library for a Saturday afternoon concert. We've arrived late and all the seats are taken. We stand in the darkened auditorium leaning against the wall. I start to worry. I know my mother cannot stand for two and a half hours. "Let's go," I whisper to her. "Sh-h-h," she says, pushing the air away with her hand. I look around. In the aisle seat next to me is a little boy, tossing about on his seat. Beside him his young mother. Next to her another little boy, and next to him the husband and father. The woman lifts the little boy in the aisle seat onto her lap and motions my mother to sit down. My mother leans over, gives the woman her most brilliant smile, and says coyly, "When you'll be eighty, and you'll want a seat at a concert, I'll come back and give you one." The woman is charmed. She turns to her husband to share her pleasure. Nothing doing. He stares balefully at my mother. Here is one Jewish son who hasn't forgotten. His response pulls me up short, reminds me of how seductive my mother has always been, how unwilling she is to part with this oldest trick of the trade, how dangerous and untrustworthy is this charm of hers.

On and on it goes. My apartment is being painted. I spend two nights on her couch. Whenever I sleep over I like to make the coffee in the morning, because she has

.en used to weak coffee and I like mine strong. Meanhile, she has become convinced that her weak coffee is the correct way to make coffee, and although she has said to me, "All right, you don't like my coffee, make it yourself," she stands over me in the kitchen and directs me to make it as she makes it.

"It's enough already," she says as I spoon coffee into the pot.

"No, it's not," I say.

"It *is*. For God's sake, enough!"

"Look for yourself, Ma. See how far short of the measuring line it is?"

She looks. The evidence is indisputable. There is not enough coffee in the pot. She turns away from me, the flat edge of her hand cutting the air in that familiar motion of dismissal.

"Ah, leave me alone," she says in deep trembling disgust.

I stare at her retreating back. That dismissiveness of hers: it will be the last thing to go. In fact, it will never go. It is the emblem of her speech, the idiom of her being, that which establishes her in her own eyes. The dismissal of others is to her the struggle to rise from the beasts, to make distinctions, to know the right and the wrong of a thing, to not think it unimportant, ever, that the point be made. Suddenly her life presses on my heart.

We are each less interested in justice than we used to be. The antagonism between us is no longer relentless. We have survived our common life, if not together at least in each other's presence, and there is a peculiar comradeship between us now. But the habit of accusation and retaliation is strong so our conversation is slightly mad these days.

"What I've lived through," my mother will sigh.

"You haven't lived through *anything*," I will retort.

"You have some damned nerve," she will shout, "to say that to me."

Silence. Anger. Separation.

Unexpectedly, her face clears and she says, "You know what farmer cheese costs now? You wouldn't believe it. Two-fifty-eight a pound."

And I'm willing, I'm willing. When I see the furious self-pity vanish from her face I allow my own to evaporate. If in the middle of a provocative exchange she says, "Well, that's the mother you got, it would have been better with another one, too damned bad this is the one you got," and I nod, "You can say that again," we both start laughing at the same time. Neither one of us, it seems, wishes to remain belligerent one sentence longer than the other. We are, I think, equally amazed that we have lived long enough to be responsive for whole minutes at a time simply to being in the world together, rather than concentrating on what each of us is or is not getting from the other.

But it has no staying power, this undreamed-of equanimity. It drifts, it gets lost, flashes up with unreliable vibrancy, then refuses to appear when most needed, or puts in an appearance with its strength much reduced. The state of affairs between us is volatile. Flux is now our daily truth. The instability is an astonishment, shot through with mystery and promise. We are no longer nose to nose, she and

I. A degree of distance has been permanently achieved. I glimpse the joys of detachment. This little bit of space provides me with the intermittent but useful excitement that comes of believing I begin and end with myself.

It is August: New York under siege. A mountain of airless heat presses down on the streets of the city. Not a bit of summer sensuality in this heat. This heat is only oppressive.

Yesterday I sat with a friend drinking iced tea in Paley Park, recovering for a moment from the exhaustion of the day. The wall of rushing water behind us created a three-sided courtyard of miraculous cool. We gazed out at the street shimmering only fifty feet from where we sat.

My friend and I, usually quite talkative, spoke listlessly of this and that: projected work, work in hand, a movie he had seen, a book I was reading, a mutual friend's new love affair. I thought I had been equally responsive to all of our small talk, but then my friend said to me, "You're remarkably uninterested in men."

"Why do you say that?" I asked.

"Every other woman I know, or man for that matter, if they've been without as long as you have, it's on their minds constantly. First priority. Not you. You seem never to think about it."

As he spoke I saw myself lying on a bed in late afternoon, a man's face buried in my neck, his hand moving slowly up my thigh over my hip, our bodies striped with bars of hot light coming through the window blinds. The image burned through me in seconds. I felt stunned by loss: the fun and sweetness of love, the deliciousness, the shimmer. I swallowed hard on empty air.

"No," I said. "I guess I don't."

Life is difficult: a glory and a punishment. Ideas are excitement, glamorous company. Loneliness eats into me. When the balance between struggle and self-pity is maintained I feel myself one of the Odd Women—that is, I see myself on a continuum of that amazing two-hundred-year effort—and I am fortified, endowed with new spirit, new will. When the balance is lost I feel buried alive in failure and deprivation, without love or connection. Friendships are random, conflicts prevail, work is the sum of its disabilities.

Tonight I am hanging on by my fingernails, barely able to hold it all together. I sit at my mother's kitchen table, drinking coffee. We have just eaten dinner. She stands at the sink washing her dishes. We are both edgy tonight. "It's the heat," she says. The apartment is air-conditioner cool, but we both love real air too much. We have turned off the machine and opened the window. For a minute the crowded noisy avenue down below invades the room, but very quickly its rush subsides into white noise, background buzz. We return almost without a pause to our own restless gloom.

My mother is conversant with all that is on my mind. She is also familiar with the usual order of my litany of complaint: work, friends, money. This evening yesterday's

201

conversation in Paley Park seems to drift in the window on the sexy summer air, and to my own surprise I find myself saying, "It *would* be nice to have a little love right now."

I expect my mother to laugh and say, "What's with you tonight?" Instead, not even looking up from the dishes, she goes on automatic and says to me, "Well, now perhaps you can have a little sympathy for *me.*"

I look up slowly at her. "What?" I say. I'm not sure I have heard right. "What was that you said?"

"I said maybe you can understand *now* what my life was like when Papa died. What it's been like all these years. Now that you're suffering from the absence of love yourself, maybe you can understand."

I stare at her. I stare and I stare. Then I'm up from the table, the cup is falling over, I fly against the kitchen wall, a caged animal. The pot she's washing clatters into the sink.

"What the hell are you talking about?" I shout. "What *are* you talking about? Again love? And yet again love? Am I never to hear anything but love from you until I die? Does my life mean nothing to you? Absolutely nothing?"

She stands at the sink rigid with terror, her eyes fixed on me, her lips white, the color draining from her face. I think I'm giving her a heart attack, but I can't stop.

"It is true," I rage on, my voice murderous now with the effort to keep it down. "I've not been successful. Neither at love, nor at work, nor at living a principled life. It is also true I made no choices, took no stands, stumbled into my life because I was angry and jealous of the world

202

beyond my reach. But *still!* Don't I get any credit for spotting a good idea, Ma? That one should *try* to live one's life? Doesn't that count, Ma? That counts for nothing, Ma?"

Her fear dissolves into pity and regret. She's so pliable these days, it's heartbreaking. "No, no," she protests, "it's another world, another time. I didn't mean anything. Of *course* you get credit. All the credit in the world. Don't get so excited. I was trying to sympathize. I said the wrong thing. I don't know how to talk to you anymore."

Abruptly, the rush of words in her is halted. Another thought has attracted her attention. The line of defense swerves. "Don't you see?" she begs softly. "Love was all I had. What did I have? I had nothing. *Nothing.* And what was I *going* to have? What *could* I have? Everything you say about your life is true, I understand how true, but you have had your work, you *have* your work. And you've traveled. My God, you've traveled! You've been halfway around the world. What wouldn't I have given to travel! I had only your father's love. It was the only sweetness in my life. So I loved his love. What could I have done?"

But mutual heartbreak is not our style. "That's not good enough, Ma," I say. "You were forty-six when he died. You could have gone out into life. Other women with a lot less at their disposal did. You *wanted* to stay inside the idea of Papa's love. It's crazy! You've spent thirty years inside the idea of love. You could have had a life."

Here the conversation ends. She is done with pleading. Her face hardens. She draws herself up into remembered inflexibility. "So," she reverts to Yiddish, the language of irony and defiance. "You'll write down here on my tomb-stone: From the very beginning it was all water under the bridge."

She turns from the dishes in the sink, wipes her hands carefully on a towel, and walks past me into the living room. I stand in the kitchen looking down at the patterned linoleum on the floor, but then after a while I follow. She is lying stretched out on the couch, her arm across her forehead. I sink down into a chair not far from the couch. This couch and this chair are positioned as they were in the living room in the Bronx. It is not difficult to feel that she has been lying on this couch and I have been sitting in this chair almost the whole of our lives.

We are silent. Because we are silent the noise of the street is more compelling. It reminds me that we are not in the Bronx, we are in Manhattan: the journey has been more than a series of subway stops for each of us. Yet tonight this room is so like that other room, and the light, the failing summer light, suddenly it seems a blurred version of that other pale light, the one falling on us in the foyer.

My mother breaks the silence. In a voice remarkably free of emotion—a voice detached, curious, only wanting information—she says to me, "Why don't you go already? Why don't you walk away from my life? I'm not stopping you."

I see the light, I hear the street. I'm half in, half out.

"I know you're not, Ma."